Strangers in Black

A Young Boy's Struggle to Survive in Khmer Rouge Cambodia

Jill Max

Royal Fireworks Press
Unionville, New York

To the memory of Betty Kaiser, whose spirit lives on in the lives she touched. And to "Mok," who had the courage to share his story.

Copyright © 2006 Royal Fireworks Publishing Company, Inc.
All Rights Reserved.

Royal Fireworks Press
P.O. Box 399
41 First Avenue
Unionville, NY 10988-0399
(845) 726-4444
fax: (845) 726-3824
email: mail@rfwp.com
website: rfwp.com

ISBN: 978-0-88092-617-1

Printed and bound in Unionville, New York, on acid-free paper
using vegetable-based inks at the Royal Fireworks facility.

Publisher: Dr. T.M. Kemnitz
Editor: Jennifer Ault
Book and Cover Designer: Kerri Ann Ruhl
Cover Art: Thomas Giana

19mr19

local 363

Prologue

Chest heaving, sweat pouring into my eyes, I hugged the tree trunk. "We must be like lizards," I whispered to my cousins, Pheap and Saveun. "Like *tekahs* who dart from place to place so fast no one sees them. Wait until I've crossed the clearing before you follow."

Eyes straining to catch the sun's reflection on a rifle barrel, ears straining to hear the slightest sound, I sucked in my breath, crouched low, and bolted to the next tree. And the next. And the next. Until there were no more trees.

Bare, charred ground stretched before me. Rusted barbed wire, strung across the field by the Khmer Rouge to keep us trapped in Cambodia, blocked my way. I scanned the cratered gray mile of minefield littered with broken, red-splotched bodies that would be my stepping stones to freedom.

Listening for gunshots, I waited for the girls to catch up with me. The only sound invading the silence was a baby wailing. It was an infant's cry, too young to be Tha's. My sister Luon and the baby are still okay, I assured myself.

Finally, they were beside me. Pheap and Saveun pressed against me, their labored breathing mingling. Tha, tied securely in Luon's *krama*, was asleep.

We gazed at the tranquil greenbelt beyond the minefield. Luon's broken teeth showed for an instant as a smile in her sunken face. "That's Thailand," she whispered.

Watching Saveun rub the angry red scars on her neck, I thought of all that had happened to us in the past four years—and all we'd lost: Tiny Sinoeun, Veun, my friend Khoy, Mir Ton, our farm, my mother in Vietnam. Remembering life before the strangers in black came, I wondered how we had come to be here—scared and starving, hiding, waiting for dark to escape to Thailand.

Chapter One
1975: Strangers in Black

The first time I saw a Khmer Rouge soldier, I was at the marketplace with my sister Luon. We had just unloaded our banana leaves and milkfruit from the rickety old town bus. It hadn't been an easy ride, perched on a reed basket that was wedged between a chicken coop and a sow with her litter. The piglets, smelling the ripe fruit, kept digging their noses into our baskets. Between swatting them, shooing chicks, and trying to stay on the jostling bus, it had been a long, bumpy ride to Big Bor.

"I'll carry the fruit," I said. Though I was small for my nine years, I was strong. I settled a bamboo pole on my shoulders, and Luon hung baskets of fruit on the ends.

"Let's go, Mok," she said. "It's almost daylight. The market will be busy already." Balancing a bundle of banana leaves on her head, she started off.

We passed women with wooden yokes across their shoulders. On one end of the yokes hung a charcoal brazier, balanced on the other end by cooking pots and produce. "Fried bananas! Sizzling rice soup! Rice cakes!" they called. My stomach rumbled with hunger as the smell of fish cooked over a charcoal fire wafted past, carried by the curling black smoke that followed them.

I followed Luon as she pushed her way toward a jungle of crowded stalls in the center of the market, where vendors beckoned shoppers in a jumble of Chinese, French, Vietnamese, and Khmer. There, under a canopy of braided palm fronds, farmers gathered to sell their produce and livestock.

"Mok!" My friend Khoy ducked under a line of crispy fried chickens hanging by their feet. "Ma gave me some *riel*," he said, waving a fistful of money. "Do you want to see the shadow play from Phnom Penh?"

Once or twice a year, a shadow play would come to Bor. While the players made tiny paper figures dance in front of a lighted screen, they sang songs and made up stories.

"Can I go, Luon?" I asked anxiously.

Luon sighed. "We have to sell all this fruit today, or it will spoil. If we make enough *riel* from selling the fruit, you may have a few *sen* to go to the shadow play."

"We can sell it in no time," said Khoy. "I'll help."

I set down the bamboo pole and grabbed a basket full of fruit. "Let's go to the *wat*," I said, hearing the sound of the monks' metal drum. "People are always hungry after they've been to the temple."

Built on stilts, the *wat* was the tallest building in the village. Through its open sides, we watched the orange-robed monks kneeling before a giant Buddha. *Even with my eyes closed, I would know I was at the* wat, I thought, inhaling the smoky jasmine of burning incense.

Our baskets emptied quickly as villagers visiting the temple bought fruit for the monks and offerings for the dead.

"Look! Someone has tied a duck to one of the graves," said Khoy. "Let's let it loose."

"We might get caught," I said.

"But they won't know who we are," assured Khoy, taking off his *krama* and wrapping the blue cloth around his face like a bandit. "Besides, the old man who guards the graves is asleep under that tree."

While Khoy kept an eye on the old man, I sneaked over to untie the duck. The duck started quacking. The old man's eyes opened.

"What's going on?" he shouted, struggling to his feet.

Khoy quacked and flapped his arms. The old man couldn't see very well and chased after him. Khoy dodged behind a statue and ran out of the graveyard. The old man stood in front of the gate, trying to locate the noisy duck.

I grabbed the duck and clamped its beak shut. I knew that if I could sneak past the old man, I'd be safe. Once I was out of the graveyard, he'd never be able to catch me.

I inched my way around the graves. There was only one shrine between the old man and me when the duck pulled its beak loose and quacked. The old man heard it and ran toward me, his white beard bouncing, spittle flying out of his mouth. I bent down and darted toward the gate behind him.

Snap! My head jerked back. The old man had hold of my hair. Gritting my teeth, I twisted free.

"You got the duck!" Khoy laughed, clutching his sides as I ran up to him safely outside the graveyard. "But look what he got!" The old man stood just outside the gate, yelling and waving a fistful of my hair.

I rubbed my head. "Come on, or we'll miss the play," I said, tossing the duck back into the graveyard.

"I'll race you," said Khoy.

I pretended to stumble at the start and then didn't run my fastest. It made Khoy mad when I always won. I chased him through the marketplace. A couple of performers were out in front of a shop, beckoning people inside to see the shadow play. I sped up, not wanting to be late, and almost bumped into Khoy, who had stopped short in front of me. I started to yell at him, but then I saw what had made him stop.

Dressed in black, red-checkered *kramas* knotted around their heads and with rifles strapped across their chests, a line of stony-faced, dark-skinned soldiers marched into the village. Their round, black eyes stared straight ahead, oblivious to the crowds watching them.

"Khmer Rouge!" Khoy whispered.

We had heard stories about the legendary Khmer Rouge who lived in the jungle. These tough peasant soldiers and their fearless leader, Pol Pot, had fought for years to oust the corrupt government of President Lon Nol. To gain support, the Khmer Rouge had promised that they would reinstate our beloved Prince Sihanouk to power.

An old man guiding an oxcart struggled to pull the cart off the road so the soldiers could pass by. The ox balked.

One of the soldiers prodded the beast from behind with his rifle.

"Look at that gun!" I said.

"I'll bet it's an AK-47 or an M16," said Khoy.

"It's an M16," I said, "just like my uncle's."

Falling into step behind the soldiers, we examined their uniforms, from their ragged tunics to the pants rolled up to their knees. Their legs and feet were streaked with mud. Their sandals, cut from tires and tied with rags, made a slapping sound on the dirt road as they marched through the village.

"Phew!" hissed Khoy, holding his nose. "I'll bet they never take baths!"

Just then an old woman broke through the crowd. "Peace at last!" she cried, falling at the feet of the soldiers. "Lon Nol has been defeated. We're saved! Long live Pol Pot! Hooray for the Khmer Rouge!"

On all sides, people took up the cry. Khoy tossed the last of the fruit to the soldiers. Clapping and shouting, we joined the excited throng weaving its way down the road.

Out of nowhere, a hand pulled me out of the cheering crowd. "We're going home," said Luon quietly. My objections were squelched by the solemn expression on her face.

It was a long, silent walk back to Small Bor. When we arrived home, my cousins, Pheap and Saveun, rushed out to greet us. "We have a surprise!" the little girls squealed. "Ba is home from Battambang!"

Mir Ton stepped out of the house. Though he was Luon's husband, I called him *mir*, or uncle, instead of brother-in-law out of respect. He was dressed in a white tunic with a blue and orange *sampot* wrapped around his waist. The expression on his face was as serious as Luon's.

Sampeihing in the traditional Cambodian fashion, Luon pressed her hands together and bowed. "I'm glad you're here," she said.

While Luon brewed a pot of tea, she and Mir Ton spoke in quiet tones. "The Khmer Rouge have come," she said.

"After five years of civil war, President Lon Nol is defeated," said Mir Ton. "The bribery, kidnapping, and tyranny that he called 'government' have come to an end. Finally, after all these years of fighting, we will have peace. Our Republican Army will work with Pol Pot and his Khmer Rouge soldiers to rebuild the country."

"Everyone in the village is cheering and waving white flags," said Luon. "They've all gone crazy."

"That's how it was in Battambang, too," said Mir Ton. "The Khmer Rouge tore open the shops. People stampeded the marketplace, scavenging everything they could find. The city is in chaos. Cars with loudspeakers patrol the streets, broadcasting messages that the Americans are going to bomb the city and everyone must leave. I came as quickly as I could."

"Will we be safe here?" asked Luon.

"I don't know," said Mir Ton.

From the doorway, I watched my cousins chasing chickens while confused thoughts tumbled through my mind. *Would the Americans bomb us, too?* I wondered. *Would we have to leave? And if so, could we return home to Vietnam and our family?*

That night the village was lit up like a New Year's celebration. Paper lanterns were strung from pole to pole, and children ran through the streets banging pots. "Long live peace!" villagers shouted, waving white flags. Young people sang and danced while the elderly played cards and gambled.

Friends and neighbors called us to join them. "Rice is flowing in the streets! The Khmer Rouge have opened the shops! Everything belongs to everyone now!"

From behind our bamboo fence, Pheap, Saveun, and I watched them rush past. "Can we go, too?" asked Saveun.

"Things are not always as they seem," said Mir Ton. "We will wait and see."

What would usually have been a festive dinner celebrating Mir Ton's return was instead a hasty meal of fish paste and rice. Taking their cue from the adults, Pheap and Saveun were quiet. Chopsticks clicked against the sides of our bowls in a strange rhythm, and martial music blared from the radio.

After dinner, while Luon and Mir Ton listened for news bulletins, I put my cousins to bed and settled onto my sleeping mat.

Finally, an announcer's voice broke through the music. "Attention all officers of the Republican Army. We ask you to assist the revolutionary organization. Help train Khmer Rouge soldiers to drive armored trucks and pilot aircraft, operate radios and clear minefields. Our soldiers are ignorant and do not know how to do any of these things. Assemble your arms, and report to your command post before 8:00 a.m. tomorrow, April 18." As abruptly as it began, the voice died.

"What will happen now?" asked Luon. The sound of fear in her voice frightened me.

"The war has ended," explained Mir Ton. "I'll help with the restructuring. Now that the fighting is over, you and the children will be safe."

"Should we send Mok home?" Luon asked.

I squeezed my eyes shut and hoped Mir Ton would say that the war in Vietnam was over, too. I missed my mother.

"No," said Mir Ton. "It's still too dangerous. Besides, with me gone, you need Mok's help with the farm. Though Saveun thinks she's grown, she's only seven, and Pheap is still a baby. We must try to sleep now. The days ahead will be difficult for all of us."

Long into the night, I listened to the rejoicing villagers and watched the light from the lanterns play across the sleeping girls' faces. I wondered why, when everyone else in Bor was celebrating the victory of the soldiers in black, Luon and Mir Ton were so somber, and why the radio was on when all we could hear was static.

Chapter Two

Leaving Home

I woke up early the next morning. I wanted to sneak into town and search through the leftovers from the previous night's celebration. If I was lucky, I might find candy, a *sen* or two, or some unexploded fireworks.

Mir Ton was up, too, and dressed in full parade uniform. His chest was covered with medals. His sword hung at his side.

"Why are you in your uniform, Mir Ton?" I asked him.

"I must return to Battambang," he answered. "It's my duty to help the Khmer Rouge."

"But you were fighting against them," I said, trying to understand.

"I am an officer in the Republican Army," explained Mir Ton. "Even though I don't believe that Lon Nol was a good president, it was my job as a soldier to support him."

"But he's not president anymore," I said.

"That's true," said Mir Ton. "The Khmer Rouge have won the war. Cambodia will be a communist country now. We will learn to live by their ways. At least we'll have peace and be working toward the same goal of rebuilding our war-torn country."

"What is *communist*?" I asked.

"In a communist country, everybody is equal," said Mir Ton. "There will no longer be rich people like Lon Nol who prosper while others are homeless and starving. Everyone will have a place to live and plenty to eat."

"Do Ma and the rest of the family know what's happening?" I asked.

"The Khmer Rouge are very proud of their victory," Mir Ton said. "I'm sure the whole world has heard the news."

"Ma will be frightened for us," I told him.

"I will send a telegram from Battambang so she won't worry," said Mir Ton. "Now, you must do something for me. Help Luon and take care of the girls until I return."

Uniform jacket stretched taut against his broad, muscular back, Mir Ton marched down the road toward Battambang. I watched until he was just an olive green dot in the distance.

After Mir Ton left, Luon kept the house dark. Friends came and went at odd hours; our spirits rose and fell with each new rumor.

On the third day of wondering, a Khmer Rouge soldier came to the house, demanding to see the head of the family.

"Where are your guns?" he asked, pushing past Luon.

"We have no guns," Luon answered.

The soldier searched everything, throwing aside our sleeping mats, dumping out baskets of food. "Where is your husband?" he demanded.

Luon looked straight into the soldier's eyes. "He's in Battambang," she said.

"You must come to the village at once," ordered the soldier.

When he left, Pheap and Saveun hid their faces in Luon's sarong and cried.

The village was a shambles. Shops were ripped apart, and goods strewn on the street. Dogs prowled through the wreckage, scavenging for food.

Silently, the villagers gathered in front of the *wat*. The monks had vanished; only the smoky jasmine scent remained. Khmer Rouge soldiers had taken over the temple. Sleeping mats and bundles littered the floor. The stone Buddha, usually surrounded by flowers and food offerings, was draped with guns and ammunition belts.

"Comrades!" a soldier shouted from the back of a truck. "Years of war have ravaged our country. The wicked Lon Nol, who stole food from your mouths and broke your backs, is gone. His reign of terror is over."

"But Ba is a soldier in Lon Nol's army," protested Saveun.

"Shhhh!" hissed Luon. "Don't speak of your father!"

"Pol Pot is the rescuer of the people," the soldier continued. "Return home. Pack only what you need for a few days. Tomorrow you will go to a new place where we will work together to rebuild our homeland for *Angka*."

Pheap tugged at Luon's sleeve. "What's *Angka*?" she asked.

"*Angka* means 'organization,'" said Luon. "That's what the new government calls itself."

All around us, people were grumbling. "What will happen to our homes? Our animals? Our crops?" they protested. "What will we eat?"

"*Angka* will provide!" shouted the soldier. "You will be given food, a place to sleep, and land. There's no need for concern. *Angka* will provide! Long live Kampuchea!"

Luon began packing as soon as we got home. She sent me to the orchard to pick all the fruit I could find. I was loading it into baskets when Khoy found me.

"We're not going," he announced. "My father says that if we leave, vandals will steal everything and destroy our home. Ma's been crying all day, begging him to take us to her brother's house in the mountains. She's afraid the soldiers will hurt us. Ba just laughs at her. He says the Khmer Rouge are here to save us from Lon Nol."

"Maybe Luon will let us stay, too," I said hopefully.

I waited all afternoon for a chance to talk to Luon. That night, when the girls were finally asleep, I found her sewing by the fire.

"We don't have to leave," I said, watching her pull the needle through the red sarong she was mending. "Khoy's family is staying. I will take care of you and the girls until Mir Ton returns."

"You're a brave boy, Mok," said Luon, "but you're no match for the soldiers' guns. We must do what they say." Pulling a brooch from her pocket, she pried loose the red and blue stones embedded in it. "These jewels are very valuable," she said, slipping them into the hem of the dress. "You must never tell where they're hidden. Someday they will help us."

When the soldiers came, we were ready. Luon had loaded the cart with clothing, pots, pans, fifty pounds of rice, dried fish, and all the fruit it would hold. I carried the crates of squawking chickens balanced on a bamboo pole. Pheap and Saveun had sleeping mats tied on their backs.

"How is Ba going to know where we are?" asked Saveun.

"I left a note for him," Luon told her. "Mir Ton will find us no matter where we are."

We joined a group of our neighbors already waiting to go. Everyone was walking, pushing wagons, pulling carts. Many, like me, carried chickens and ducks; others tugged pigs behind them. A few of the wealthier had oxen to carry their belongings.

On the way out of town, we passed Khoy's house. "Please, let me say goodbye to Khoy," I begged Luon.

Before she could stop me, I ran to the house. "Khoy! Khoy!" I called, pounding on the door.

A neighbor woman shouted at me. "They're gone! Pol Pot's men came. They loaded the whole family with their hands tied on a truck and took them away. Even all their money couldn't save them."

With a heavy heart, I rejoined Luon and the girls.

Chapter Three
I Am Your Mother

The highway to Battambang was jammed with people—thousands of us forced to leave our homes. We walked and walked. After a short time, Pheap and Saveun were too tired to walk. Luon lifted them into the cart. There was no room for me, so I followed behind.

The highway was paved with blacktop. It blistered my bare feet and cut into my skin.

"Keep going," my sister urged.

"My feet can't walk any farther," I cried. But I kept going. My head was so full of noise that it hurt: children crying, families calling out to one another, dogs barking, fowl squawking. Soldiers were everywhere, riding in trucks. Whenever the trucks came, people became silent, moving to the side to let them pass.

The soldiers all looked the same. They were young—not much older than I. Their hair was cut short, even the girls. And they all had broad, flat noses and the same black, round eyes that stared at you without seeing. Pheap called them "fish eyes."

About twenty kilometers out of town, we smelled something.

"Someone's cooking fish," said Saveun.

As we drew closer, the smell grew stronger. It was a foul odor, like no other I had ever smelled—a smell so bad it made my eyes water. We pulled our *kramas* over our faces.

It wasn't long before we saw where the smell was coming from. Piled on the side of the road were mounds of Republican Army officers, their hands tied behind their backs—dead, bloated, decaying soldiers, purple and green and black.

I shook with fear. I couldn't take my eyes off the red stars on the soldiers' uniforms. A part of me knew that Mir Ton would never see the note we'd left for him. Several children stood staring at the bodies, weeping. A truck stopped beside them. "Why are you crying?" the soldiers yelled. "These people were your enemies!"

Frightened by the soldiers, the children cried louder. The soldiers raised their rifles and pointed them at the children. "If you don't stop crying, we'll shoot you, too!" they threatened.

"Cover your eyes," said Luon, hugging the girls to her breast.

A woman broke through the crowd and hustled the children away, melting into the melee of carts, bicycles, and people.

We hurried away, too, pushing the cart as fast as we could. It was after dark before the soldiers allowed us to stop for the night. Many people camped right on the road or slept in open ditches; others scrambled for prime locations under trees. We stopped at a vacant spot where a scraggly bush provided a little shelter. While Saveun and I foraged through the field for twigs to start a fire, Pheap scraped a bare place in the dirt with her hands and made a game of arranging rocks in a circle around it.

"Look!" called out a fishmonger from Big Bor. "The wife of an officer is sleeping under a cart!" She was pointing at Luon.

My sister's eyes flashed a mixture of fear and anger. "Please, don't call me that," Luon said, bending to fill our pot with water. "Please leave us alone."

Later, I asked Luon why the woman had upset her. "You saw the bodies of the soldiers piled along the road," she said. "It isn't safe to be the family of a Republican soldier."

That night, Luon sat alone by the smoldering fire. She made a pyre of her wedding chopsticks. Speechless, I watched her take all our *riel* and lay them on the coals. Then, one by one, she fed the family photographs to the pyre. Her eyes shone with tears as the flames licked at the familiar faces.

Before dawn, the soldiers ordered us to rise and start walking. We walked all that day, the next day, and the day after that. All of the days were the same. After a while, my feet hurt so badly that they stopped hurting, numb from the pain.

The dead were our constant companions. Once, we passed a soldier lying by the side of the road, his legs still wrapped around his motorcycle. Bullets had blown his chest apart. His blank eyes stared, unable to blink away the swarming flies.

I stopped seeing the bodies littering the road, stopped hearing the babies crying for food, stopped smelling the smell of thousands of people crushed together. All I could do was put one foot in front of the other, like a zombie.

The supplies we had brought from the farm were running low. The fruit was gone, as were the chickens. While Luon mixed the last bit of dried fish with peppers and rice, Saveun and I struggled to wrap our fingers, used to chopsticks, around the crude Khmer spoons.

We had just started eating when a patrol marched through the camps. Without giving us time to gather our belongings, they shoved us toward an abandoned factory.

I craned my neck to see into the dimly lit building. We were standing in a long line. At the front of the line were three soldiers sitting at a table. As people approached the table, either alone or in family groups, they were questioned, then dismissed. Some were told to wait, others to leave.

My sister whispered to Pheap and Saveun. Then she grasped my hand, and, pulling me so close that I could smell the peppers on her breath, she hissed, "Listen to me. From now on, I am your mother."

I shook my head in protest. Luon's nails dug into my wrists. "They will take you from me and send you off with strangers if you don't do what I say," she said. "You are my son now, and you are only six. Understand? Your cousins are your sisters. We are a family." She looked fiercely into my eyes. "Who am I?" she demanded.

I hesitated. Her nails dug deeper into my flesh. "Ma," I whispered.

"Never forget that!" she said. "No matter who asks you, say the same thing."

When our time came at the front of the line, the soldiers asked my sister who we were and where we came from.

"I'm from Bor," answered Luon.

"Where is your husband?"

"He is dead."

"Was he a soldier?"

"He was a farmer."

I kept my face blank, not betraying Luon's lies. "What do you do?" the soldier demanded.

"I'm a farmer," said Luon. A soldier grabbed her hands and turned them over, rubbing at the dirt and ridges on her palms. "You don't believe me? Look at this." She thrust a mangled index finger toward him. "It was smashed by a thresher."

They asked my cousins the same questions. Saveun answered the same; Pheap could only whimper.

When my turn came, my sister stepped in front of me. "He knows nothing. There's something wrong in his head. He's not right, but he works hard."

Imitating the idiot boy who scaled fish in the market, I let my mouth fall open in a stupid grin and forced my eyes upward.

The soldier grimaced. "That's all," he said and motioned for us to leave.

It wasn't until the building was far behind that I dared ask Luon a question. "Why did the soldiers make those other people stay?"

"Because they admitted to being soldier's families," explained Luon, "or having jobs with the government or being educated."

"Ba is a soldier," said Saveun.

"And there are dead soldiers everywhere," said Luon. "I don't know what they'll do with the soldiers' families."

That night when we camped, we made a bigger fire than usual. Luon boiled all of our clothes with tree root until they were black. I knew it was best if we looked like Khmer Rouge. Still, when she took out her knife, a lump filled my throat. I winced as my cousins' silky black hair fell to the ground.

Chapter Four

The Palace Dancers

The soldiers forced us to keep moving. The old people, too tired or sick to walk, collapsed and were dragged to the side of the road in order to keep the stream of people flowing. Lying amid the growing piles of clothing and household goods, they cried out for help or waited for death.

At first, we searched abandoned bundles for food and valuables, but most had been picked over. Once, Pheap found a mirror, a jar of rice powder, and lipstick in a flowered silk purse. She begged until Luon let her keep them. After a while, however, we stopped searching for valuables. Even if we found something we wanted, we were too tired to carry it.

Just outside of Treng, the highway crossed some railroad tracks. The wheel of our cart lodged between the ties. We tried to rock it loose, but it wouldn't budge. A family of city people saw us struggling and came over to help. They got behind the cart and pushed. With a painful crack, the wheel broke off, and the cart crashed to the ground. Pheap and Saveun tumbled onto the tracks behind it, and Pheap cut her forehead. Blood was running down her face, but Luon didn't notice it. She was on her knees trying to put the wheel back on the cart. I tore a corner off of my shirt and bandaged

Pheap's head. Then I tried to help Luon, but the cart was too badly broken.

"Keep moving!" shouted the soldiers.

Luon and I unloaded the cart, packing our belongings into our *kramas* and tying them to our backs. We pushed the cart off the road and started walking. Pheap and Saveun tired easily, so Luon and I took turns carrying them. Saveun, because she was older, was left to guard Luon's pack while Luon carried Pheap a short way. When we stopped, Luon rested, watching Pheap and my pack while I doubled back to pick up Luon's pack and then Saveun. Slowly, in this tedious manner, we made our way to Treng.

Treng looked a lot like Small Bor: houses deserted, shops ravaged. Cars with their tires gone were heaped at the side of the road. Any hope we had of finding food and shelter was destroyed.

Treng was overrun with refugees from the city of Battambang. These refugees were different from us. The women wore gold and silver-patterned sarongs, their cloth slippers stiff with dried mud. The men dressed Western-style, with ties and hard, closed-toed shoes. Many carried their belongings on bicycles or motorcycles. Others had hired *cyclo-pousses*. We moved quickly aside when one of these rickety bicycles rumbled past, its rickshaw heaped with rich people's belongings. Some of the city people even pushed trucks that no longer ran, loaded with television sets and refrigerators.

Soldiers in jeeps patrolled the streets, shouting through bullhorns, harassing the refugees. Rich people tried to bribe the soldiers so they would leave them in peace.

"Lon Nol's money is only good for lighting cigarettes!" the soldiers laughed as they burned the *riel*. Randomly, they ransacked people's belongings for cameras and radios that they didn't know how to operate, watches and fountain pens that they didn't know how to use.

"Stop, China boy!" shouted a soldier, leaping onto the street. He grabbed a boy's long braid and yanked him off his scooter. Too scared to resist, the boy crawled into the shadows. The soldier mounted the scooter. When he couldn't start the motor, he pushed it and tried to pop the clutch. The other soldiers in the jeep laughed at him. Their taunts made his face burn red. He threw the scooter into the dirt. "Worthless foreign trash!" he shouted, blasting it full of holes with his machine gun.

Saveun and I left Luon to guard our belongings while we searched for food. We found a rice bag in the road that must have fallen from a cart. Most of the rice was scattered in the dirt. We knelt down and started picking up the grains.

Suddenly, I felt a gun pointed at my head. I was too frightened to move.

Saveun started screaming, "Don't kill my uncle! Don't kill my uncle!"

Maybe the soldier had a sister or a daughter like Saveun because he put his gun away. "Don't take any more food," he warned. "It belongs to *Angka*. The next soldier may not be so forgiving."

The Khmer Rouge forbade us to enter any buildings. People were forced to set up camp anywhere there was an empty spot: in ditches and doorways, under cars and houses.

Day and night we were bombarded with martial music blaring from loudspeakers mounted on poles throughout the town. The cries of people searching for loved ones were endless: "Have you seen a young girl?" "Have you seen my mother?" "Grandmother?" "Grandfather?" "Have you seen my brother?" Warmed by our campfire fed with table legs, I thanked Buddha that our family was together.

Before sunrise, we were awakened by bullhorns.

"People of Kampuchea! You are being relocated. You will be given land to grow rice for *Angka*. During Lon Nol's regime, greedy soldiers ate all the rice, and we went hungry. Now we will work together toward a glorious future for everyone."

"We're hungry now!" someone shouted.

"When you get to the camp," continued the soldier, "you will have rice and fruit and fish paste—all you can eat. *Angka* will provide. Get ready to go!"

Not everyone was happy about this move. Some people talked about escaping north to Thailand. Others talked about going into the jungle and hiding. Still others decided to head for the river where at least there would be no shortage of food and water.

"Let's go to the river," I said to Luon, the thought of fresh fish making my mouth water.

"People who go to the river never come back," warned Luon. So we joined the swarm of people going to the camp. Just ahead of us were five girls with flowered boxes tied to their backs. Each wore a different-colored sarong. The silk hugged their legs and hips. Their bodies swayed, and their arms floated upward with each small step.

"They're dancers," Luon informed us. "Once, when your father and I were in Phnom Penh, we saw them perform. It was at the Palace, and Prince Sihanouk was there. I'll never forget their slow, graceful motions, like flowers. They are taught to dance when they are tiny like you, Pheap, and they practice all their lives. Each of the dancers' steps, each movement of their hands, has a meaning."

"What did the palace dancers wear?" asked Saveun.

"Their costumes were encrusted with thousands of sequins that sparkled and shimmered," said Luon in a faraway voice. "Some of them wore cone-shaped headdresses. In one dance, they wore masks that looked like giant birds and monkeys."

My cousins and I couldn't stop ourselves. We stared at the doll-like creatures until we lost them in the crowd.

That night we saw the dancers again, camped under a mangrove tree. The one dressed in purple took a golden scarf from her box and spread it on the ground. The others sat beside her.

"They don't have anything to eat," I said to Luon.

"Can I give them my rice?" asked Saveun.

"This is all we have," said Luon. "If you give yours away, you'll have none for later."

No sooner had she said the words than the three of us were on our way. We couldn't wait to get a closer look at the doll-dancers.

But before we reached them, a truckful of soldiers pulled up in front of us, and the soldiers jumped out. We heard screaming. When we peeked around the truck, the soldiers were ripping open the flowered boxes. Turquoise, scarlet, emerald, and golden costumes covered with layers of sequins tumbled to the ground. Shoving the dancers aside, the soldiers fell upon the dresses.

The dancer in purple snatched a tiny crown from the pile. A girl-soldier jerked it from her hand. "That belongs to *Angka* now," the soldier said, putting it on.

I felt rage mounting inside me as the soldiers pried jewels from the exquisite gowns and crowns. One of the comrades wrapped himself in a sequined robe and twirled around and around; two others shoved their masked faces up to the girls, growling, snarling, and shrieking like animals. Helpless, I watched the dancers crawl through the remnants of silk, sequins, and jewels, scooping them from under the soldiers' feet. Tears etched lines through their smooth, white-powdered faces.

Finally, the soldiers left. Knowing that our presence would cause embarrassment, we placed our meager offerings beside the dancers and returned to Luon.

Chapter Five
Phnom Pong

The days passed, measured only by the kilometers we walked and the rice we ate.

"I'm dizzy," I moaned, pulling my feet through the dirt. "My head hurts, and I can't see."

"You're hungry and tired," said Luon. "We'll stop here." She forced me to gulp down some water so I wouldn't feel the hunger. I covered my head and fell into a fitful sleep. I woke up shivering. Soaked in sweat, my body throbbed with pain.

Luon went to find help. She brought back a woman who had been a nurse in Battambang.

"It's malaria," the woman declared flatly. "He needs quinine, but the Khmer Rouge have confiscated all the medicine." She cradled my face in her hands and wiped the sweat from my brow. Even her gentle ministrations stung my skin. "I have nothing to give you," she said.

Supported by Luon and the girls, I made it as far as a Khmer Rouge camp at the base of Phnom Pong. *How can they call this "Little Mountain"?* I wondered, dragging myself up the steep, narrow path. Luon helped me to a stream. I lay on my belly and dunked my head, letting the water run into my mouth and over my burning body.

"Move on," shouted a soldier, nudging me with his foot.

"My son is sick," said Luon. "Can't we stay until he's better?"

"There are too many people here already," said the soldier. "You must go to the next camp."

"We can't go farther. He barely made it this far," Luon told him. "Please, let us stay."

The soldier pulled my face up by my hair. "From the looks of him, he won't last much longer anyway. Camp over there." He pointed to a stand of brush far from other people, and even farther from the stream.

With her cooking knife, Luon cleared a space in the dense undergrowth. I slumped against a tree while she and the girls spread out our sleeping mats and started a fire.

The camp, like the mountain, was called Phnom Pong. I finally understood why it was called Little Mountain when the fog lifted and I gazed upon the enormous Cardamom Mountain Range stretching beyond it.

Hidden amid the thick, hairy vines, thorny brush, and poison ivy that shrouded Phnom Pong were fruits and berries, edible roots, tubers, and *sdow* trees. Luon learned from a woman in the camp who practiced folk medicine that *sdow* leaves are a remedy for malaria. She steeped the leaves, and I choked down as much of the vile tea as I could. Soon, my fever broke.

Chapter Six
The House that Mok Built

It didn't take long to discover that the Khmer Rouge soldiers weren't all equals. Most of them, brown and ragged, were clearly farm people like us. They called one another *met*, which means friend. They only spoke to us when they were giving orders.

But the leaders, like Comrade Muy, whose belly was big from plenty of food, wore clean, new, button-covered uniforms. They rarely came out of Khmer Rouge headquarters. When they did, everyone, even the soldiers, grew silent.

One day, Comrade Muy and two soldiers passed by our camp. I didn't think they noticed us. Later, one of the soldiers came back. "You must build a house, or you'll have to leave," he said.

We had never built a house. Other people in the camp were building shelters, so we watched and copied them. First we cleared a large area around our camp. Sweat rolled off our bodies as we hacked away the brush. We needed to get the house together as quickly as possible; the heavy, moist air was a sign that the rainy season was near.

Luon and I chopped bamboo poles and wrapped them together with vines to make a frame for the house. Pheap and Saveun tied brush into bundles for the roof. We had just finished the frame and were getting ready to add the walls when Comrade Muy stopped us. "There are enough people here," he said. "You can't stay."

Careful not to look at him, I pleaded, "The soldier told us to build a house. Please, Comrade, let us stay. Our house is almost finished."

"You new people think only of yourselves!" he said. "There are already enough people here to farm this land. *Angka* needs all of the land cultivated. You must do what's best for all. You must move!"

When he left, Luon glared at me. "Don't argue again!" she said. "Do what they say!"

So we took the house apart and carried it around the mountain, where we rebuilt it. While we were putting the roof on, the rains came. At first it only showered two or three times a day. Luckily, we got the walls up before the heavy rains started. After that I didn't have to carry water anymore. Cooking pots placed under bamboo pipes caught the runoff from the roof.

Not far from us lived a family—a mother, father, two boys, and two girls. Their house was only sticks with a grass roof. They must have been rich before they were forced to relocate because they didn't know how to find food. The starving children cried all the time. First the mother and father swelled up with big bellies and legs like tree trunks. They lay on the ground moaning, unable to walk. Then they died. After that, the children begged food from the soldiers, but it was too late. The two girls and one of the boys died. The other boy was lucky: a family took him in.

We kept to ourselves. Pheap and Saveun played and chased butterflies while Luon and I looked for food. On one of our forages, we happened upon a grove of sugar palm trees.

"Look!" I said, pointing to the bamboo pipes hanging from their trunks.

"The old owners must have sold sugar palm juice," Luon remarked.

"I'll climb up and get some," I said.

"Leave them alone," warned Luon. "It's too dangerous. They belong to the Pol Pots now."

My mouth salivated at the thought of the sugary liquid. On our farm, we had milked the sugar palm trees. We broke off a flower and hung a bamboo pipe beneath the cut to catch the juice. When boiled, the juice became a thick, sweet syrup that Luon used to make delicious candy and cakes.

On repeated trips to the grove, I saw that the bamboo pipes hadn't been moved, so I knew that no one was tending the trees. My desire to taste the sweet juice overcame caution, and I dared to climb the palm trees. To my disappointment, most of the cuts in the trunks had scabbed over, and the pipes were empty.

I'd saved the largest tree for last. I scaled the trunk. My reward was a full pipe. Greedily, I lifted it to my lips and took a sip of the nectar.

Thump! Something hit my nose. I thought a flower must have fallen into the pipe. To my surprise, instead of a flower,

I fished out a bat, dizzy from drinking too much sugar. That night's meal of bat and sugar palm juice was a feast!

In the damp, loamy recesses of the jungle grew mushrooms of all kinds—some as big as my head, others tiny buttons. Plenty of people died from eating poisonous varieties. Fortunately, Luon knew about some of the mushrooms because we had them on our farm. When we saw someone eat an unfamiliar kind, we watched and waited to see if that person lived.

Once, I saw one of the men from camp filling his pockets with pumpkin-colored mushrooms that grew out of a decaying tree stump.

"Take some," he said. "They're good."

Pretending to be scared, I shook my head and ran away. Later that night, the man doubled up in pain, with vomiting and diarrhea at the same time. "Help me, Buddha!" he screamed. By morning, he was dead.

Chapter Seven
Meetings

The first time I went to a Khmer Rouge meeting, I didn't know what it was. Soldiers told Luon that everyone in the family had to go, so we joined the other families walking toward the center of camp.

At first we all just stood around. Then one of the soldiers told us to sit down in rows. The soldiers walked up and down the rows, tapping their guns, looking us over. *Were they counting us? Were they looking for someone?* The longer we sat, the more worried I became.

The soldiers' black shirts were covered with buttons— gold, silver, ivory. I couldn't keep my eyes off them. One of the soldiers caught me staring. She switched rows and walked so close to me that her pants brushed my arm. She stopped. I could feel her eyes boring into my head and smell the sweat-dampened rings under her arms. Concentrating on the dirt between my toes, I held my breath until she finally moved on.

After we'd been sitting for about an hour, Comrade Muy came. "It is time to show *Angka* what good workers we are," he said. "We will build a cafeteria. When it is finished, *Angka* will provide us with food."

The promise of full bellies urged us on. With so many people living off the land, the jungle around the camp had quickly become depleted. The trees were stripped of fruits, berries, and even edible leaves. Most of the bamboo had been chopped down for food or housing. We quickly built the cafeteria, which was nothing more than a thatched nipa palm roof supported by bamboo poles.

At one end of the cafeteria were fire pits where workers stirred pots of watery rice soup. Twice a day we lined up to receive our rations. Using condensed milk cans as measures, the cafeteria workers doled out half a can of soup to each child and a full can to each adult. This soup wasn't seasoned with herbs and full of vegetables and meat like Luon's. It had only one or two pieces of vegetable floating in it, although on a good day you could find a bit of chicken or fish. But it was better than nothing.

One day I was standing in line waiting for the day's ration when I heard soldiers laughing. A group of them were gathered in a circle. In the center was the idiot boy from the marketplace, running around, clutching a squash. One of the soldiers was crouched low. Over and over he lunged forward and snatched at the squash. Each time he reached out, the boy barked and snarled.

"Here, dog. Here, dog," coaxed the watching soldiers. The boy crept forward and rolled on his back. When one of the soldiers tried to pull the squash away, the boy howled. Then his tongue rolled out, and he began to pant.

The soldiers laughed louder and continued to tease the boy. "Let him keep it," they said, finally tiring of the game. The boy hugged the squash tightly until the soldiers were out of sight. Then he bit the stem off and started eating it.

I looked ahead of me at the line of people. *If I were an idiot boy,* I thought, *I wouldn't have to wait for food.*

Chapter Eight
You Are Not Vietnamese

During the rainy season, the stream swelled over the banks, flooding the valley below. As soon as the floods receded, big trucks with Chinese writing on the side came to our camp. They were loaded with bags of seed rice. Everyone who was able was sent to scatter the seeds.

At the nightly meetings, we tried to ignore the hunger pangs in our bellies while the leaders filled us with propaganda instead of food. One after the other, they spoke, each trying to find different ways of saying the same things: "Life has been hard for the Khmer Rouge soldiers in the jungle." "We must all work hard to grow rice for *Angka*." "The Chinese, Americans, French, and Vietnamese have exploited Kampuchea." "See how we brave and courageous Khmer Rouge soldiers drove out these foreign oppressors!"

I propped my elbows on my knees and held my eyelids open with my fingers. I knew that if the leaders caught me dozing, I would be singled out for punishment.

"You there," said Comrade Muy, pointing to a man with glasses sitting at the back of the room. "What good are those glasses? They are the product of foreign invaders."

"I need them to see," said the man.

Comrade Muy pulled the glasses off the man's face. "Can you see my hand?" he demanded.

"Yes," the man said.

"Then you don't need these glasses," said Comrade Muy, crushing them with his sandal. "Glasses are only good for reading foreign lies."

Copying Comrade Muy, others in the room removed their glasses and smashed them.

Sometimes only the grownups had to go to the meetings. Then I stayed home with Pheap and Saveun. With so little food, they were too tired to play. All they wanted to do was lie on their mats.

While they slept, I remembered how things had been before the Khmer Rouge. I pulled a charred piece of wood from the fire and held it in my hands. Though completely burned, it was still hot. I tossed it back and forth. It made my hands black. Holding the wood like a pen, I drew a picture of our farm. I drew pictures of Mir Ton, Khoy, and my mother. I drew figures that the monks had taught me.

"What are you doing?"

I jumped at the sound of Luon's voice. Her face was twisted in horror. She tore the stick from my hand and took the strips of bark I'd drawn on, even the one with the pictures of the family, and threw them into the fire. Grabbing me by the shoulders, she shook me until my neck ached from snapping back and forth. With clenched teeth, only her lips moving, she said, "Never draw again! Never write!" She held her hands over my ears. Tears ran down her face like rain. "You do not hear Vietnamese," she said. Then she closed my eyes with her fingers. "You no longer see Vietnamese. You are only Cambodian now—a stupid Cambodian farm boy. Forget everything else. Now you know only this place. You speak only Khmer. Forget everything from before, or we will all be killed."

I tried to shut my mind, but I couldn't shut my heart. Out of a distant time, my mother's voice, clear and true, lulled me to sleep with a Vietnamese lullaby.

Chapter Nine

Working in the Rice Paddies

Once the rice seeds sprouted, we had to separate them. We got up before the sun and walked in darkness to the flooded lowlands, where we stood all day in water almost to our knees, planting fistfuls of seedlings one by one in the muddy paddy. I walked backwards, my body bent over until it ached. Sometimes it burned with pain, but I didn't stop. Soldiers guarded us, standing on the walls of dirt surrounding the paddy. If we were caught resting, our rations were cut.

Just when the sun was starting to get hot, the women from the cafeteria brought watery rice soup—our first meal of the day. I crawled out of the paddy and fell in a heap on the dike. Then I saw my legs.

"Aieee!" I cried. Stuck to my legs were black, slimy, slug-like creatures.

"They're leeches," Luon told me. "Get them off."

I tried to brush them off, but they held fast. A man next to me reached over and took one of the leeches between his fingers. He yanked it off. Blood spurted out. I screamed, clutching my leg.

"The paddies are full of leeches," he said. "They attach themselves to your body and suck your blood. You'd better take the others off, or they'll make you sick."

I held in my pain while Luon pulled off the rest of the leeches.

Planting the seedlings was just the beginning. Day after day, we tended the paddies to keep the weeds from choking the tender shoots. Growing rice was more difficult than working the farm in Small Bor. There, the mango and banana trees grew wild. All we had to do was pick the fruit when it was ripe.

Shrimp and crab thrived in the murky paddy water. If we were lucky—and fast enough—we'd catch one and roll it in the cuff of our pants to eat later.

The seedlings grew. Soon the valley was a green-checkered blanket of rice stalks. When the plants were waist-high, we broke holes in the dikes with our hands to let the water drain. If we didn't do that, the crop would rot, and we'd have no rice.

The trucks bringing food stopped coming. Though we continued going to the cafeteria for meals, the watery soup was not enough to keep us alive. We began to supplement our meager diet by foraging.

"Everything belongs to everyone," the leaders said. "Taking food from the jungle is stealing. Thieves will be punished."

But our instinct to survive was stronger than the Pol Pots' threats. Secretly, every edible leaf, root, and flower around the base of Phnom Pong was scavenged. We dug desperately for grubs and worms, shoving anything we thought might stop the gnawing hunger pains into our mouths.

No sooner did we eat something than it came out the other end. Guava tree bark tea was the only thing we knew that would stop the cramping and diarrhea. In front of every hut, balanced on a triangle of stones, was a boiling pot of this gray-brown, foul-tasting brew. These pots of tea were useful in another way, too. Because everyone had one, the soldiers didn't check them, and we could sneak food into the tea and cook it right under their noses.

Saveun and I slept in the doorway so that we could be close to the bushes when the grinding pains began. Pheap was too sick to move. Luon was gently cleaning her when she saw round, wriggling creatures in her stools. "Worms," she said, sucking in her breath.

"I thought they were something we ate," said Saveun.

Cursing softly, Luon finished with Pheap and left the hut. She returned carrying a branch from a *ktamtat* tree. It was covered with pods that looked like giant snow peas. She chewed one of the pods, took a bit of the pulp from her mouth, and forced it between Pheap's lips.

"Mok and Saveun, you eat some, too," she demanded. "The *ktamtat* pods will make the worms come out."

I thought the pods would kill me, they tasted so vile and bitter. Closing my eyes, I choked one down. Soon, the worms were gone.

Chapter Ten

Finding Frogs

I discovered a hidden spot in the forest where *ptib*, a spinach-like plant, grew. On my way to pick some one day, I saw people jumping up and down on a grassy mound, yelling to one another. I watched them, wondering what they were doing.

"I got one!" hollered a man. A tiny gray field mouse dangled limply from his hand. With so little food, a field mouse was a feast.

I joined in the mouse hunt. The mice had dug a maze of tunnels throughout the mound. A person would stand guard at each hole. Then, all at once, we'd start screaming and stomping. When the frightened mice ran out of the holes, we clubbed them. It would have been much easier to trap them in cages, but we had nothing to use for bait. Everyone shared the catch, which meant that often all I got for a day's work was a mouthful.

I soon tired of the mouse hunt. Besides, Pheap and Saveun were having better luck catching crabs and frogs. On a particularly lucky trip, my cousins and I managed to stab six frogs with our sharpened bamboo slivers. We were hurrying home with them when a Khmer Rouge boy stopped us.

"Hey, *met*," he said. "You find any frogs?"

"Yes," I said. "A few."

"I'll make you a deal," he offered. "I'll trade you a bag of rice for your frogs."

I happily handed over all the frogs.

"These belong to me now," he said. "You have to come to my house to get the rice."

I was scared to go to a Khmer Rouge house. "You get it for me," I said.

"No," said the boy. "You have to get it yourself." He laughed and ran away.

I vowed that I would never let anyone take our food again. From then on, I foraged alone. By myself, it was easier to hide whenever I saw someone.

The endless search for food took me far from camp. I was digging for roots in a strange part of the jungle when I heard voices. I dove under a bush and peeked out. In the clearing beyond, people were plowing a field. A water buffalo was harnessed to one side of a forked tree branch. Three people, taking the place of a missing water buffalo, were harnessed to the other side. An old grandmother, standing on the back of the plow, tried to guide them without falling off. *If I were them, I'd eat that water buffalo,* I thought, watching them struggle with the beast.

A stream ran through the field. The sound of the water made my throat thick. *They look like nice people,* I thought. *A family perhaps. They won't mind if I drink some water.*

I stepped into the clearing. The people stopped talking. Gingerly, I waded into the stream and knelt down. It was so quiet. *What are they doing? Will they turn me in?* "Water belongs to everyone," I repeated to keep up my courage. "Water belongs to everyone."

I wiggled my hands in the stream to clear the debris from the surface, cupped them, and bent to drink. Too late, I saw the dead man, swollen and purple. The skin on his body was peeling off like layers of parchment. Beside him was a water buffalo carcass. I felt sick to my stomach.

These are not good people, I thought, *leaving a man unburied and his ghost to wander with no place to rest. If I stay here, I'll end up like him.* I ran back into the bush.

Chapter Eleven
Don't Eat the Banana

I was searching for a lizard or a bug or a snake—anything to eat—when, out of the corner of my eye, I saw a boy about my age. He wore a nice shirt and pants, and he looked like he had lots of rice, vegetables, and fish to keep him strong. I knew that this boy was the son of a Khmer Rouge soldier. I pretended not to notice him and hoped that he would leave me alone.

I spotted a small green banana lying in the grass. It was just off the flower, nowhere near ripe, but to me it looked like a feast. I wanted to pick it up, but I could feel the boy watching me.

"Can I have that banana?" I asked the boy.

The boy only looked at me with cold, black eyes. I smoothed my torn shirt and brushed the dirt off my pants. Head lowered, I asked again, "Can I have that banana?"

Without answering, the boy brushed past me. I picked up the banana and tucked it into my shirt. I searched a few minutes more, with no success. Knowing I'd be missed if I stayed longer, I turned back.

Blocking my way was the boy and his soldier-father. I froze. The soldier took the gun from his holster. "You stole that banana!" he said. He cocked the gun and pushed it into my forehead. I stumbled backward and fell against a tree. I was sure that I was going to die.

"Please don't kill me," I pleaded. "I didn't steal the banana. It's just a little green banana, not good to eat. But I have nothing. Please don't kill me!"

The soldier pulled a rope from his pocket and tied me to the tree. Tears dripped out of my eyes. I begged the soldier, "Please don't kill me! Please let me go! I will never come back here again. If you ever see me here again, you can kill me. Please let me go now."

The hard barrel of the gun dug into my forehead. I knew the boy was watching me. I didn't care. I didn't want to die. I kept crying and begging.

Suddenly, the soldier swung his arm down and knocked the banana out of my hand. "I'll let you go this time," he said. "But if I ever see you again, I'll kill you." He put the gun back in his holster and walked away. The boy crushed the banana and followed his father.

Chapter Twelve
Mud on Their Backs

Each time Comrade Muy led a meeting, his words were the same: "See how *Angka* takes care of you. Everything belongs to everyone. If anyone is hiding food, bring it to the cafeteria. Khmer children, you are the future of *Angka*. If your parents have food, you must tell us. If they are professionals, doctors, or teachers, stand up. They will be forgiven for following the wicked ways of the foreigner. If your parents have mud on their backs, they can't see it. You must help your parents be better Khmers. Show us the mud so we can help them. *Angka* will forgive them."

"My father is hiding dried fish under his sleeping mat," a girl called out.

Comrade Muy took the girl's hand and led her to the front. "You have made *Angka* proud. You are a good Khmer. You are helping your father be a good Khmer, too."

"My father is a teacher," another child offered.

"My mother buried chickens in the jungle."

"My parents own a factory."

Night after night, children came forward. After the meetings, the soldiers visited their houses. The parents of the children who had spoken out were taken away. But Luon had taught us well—Pheap, Saveun, and I remained silent.

Chapter Thirteen
Eating Dangerously

Luon was working in the cafeteria, and she begged the soldiers to let her keep the seeds that she scraped from inside pumpkins. Afraid that someone would steal them, she kept the seeds in her pocket until they were dried and ready to plant. It wasn't long before vines were crawling all over the place. Luon watched over the plants like they were her babies. She snipped the tender tips off the new vines and hid the tiny green pumpkins under leaves so that no one would find them. One night, a Khmer Rouge soldier startled her.

"What are you doing?" he asked.

Luon flicked dirt over an exposed pumpkin and jumped to her feet. "Making the plants grow better for *Angka*," she responded quickly. "If you snap one shoot, two grow in its place. If you snap two, four grow. In no time, *Angka* will have plenty of pumpkins."

"You are a good Khmer," said the soldier. "You do honor to *Angka*."

Pheap and Saveun had become shrunken, silent skeletons. Though there were no mirrors, I knew I was one, too. At night, lying on our mats, we prayed for sleep so we could stop thinking about food.

"I can't sleep," said Pheap.

"I can almost smell Ma's fried noodles," said Saveun.

"With onions, ginger, and eel," I added, licking my cracked lips.

"I can smell it!" said Pheap.

"You're imagining things," said Luon. "Go to sleep."

"I smell it, too!" I cried. "Someone's cooking meat!"

With energy I didn't know I had, I jumped up and followed the scent, Pheap and Saveun close behind me. A group of people was clustered around a fire. Squeezing through the crowd, we made our way to the edge of the pit. Lashed to a spit was an enormous boa constrictor.

"Look at its head!" gasped Pheap. With every turn of the spit, the snake's neck lolled, its tongue bobbing in its mouth. "Are they going to eat it?"

"It might be poisonous," said Saveun, cringing. "We'd better wait and see if makes them sick."

"If we wait, it will be gone, and we'll have nothing," I pointed out.

When the snake was done, I ripped off some meat, along with the others, and we devoured it. It did not make us sick.

•   •   •

From the moment I awoke, while I worked, at meetings, my mind was consumed with thoughts of food. I constantly searched for something to eat. Grubs, worms, scorpions, spiders—things that I used to save or squish—were now dinner. Pheap and Saveun became good hunters, too. They caught crickets, snails, and ants.

Pheap caught a mouse one day while the rest of us were gone. Just as she had seen Luon do, she put it in a coconut shell to cook. The shell caught on fire, singeing the mouse. Pheap reached in and pulled it from the fire. When we returned, she was sitting on the ground. Unmindful of her burned fingertips, she had cut the raw mouse into strips and was eating it, blood, dirt, and charcoal smeared across her face.

Since the Khmer Rouge had done away with all of the doctors and nurses, we turned to "witch doctors," called Kru Khmers, for remedies. The Kru Khmer in our camp was so old that his flesh was speckled brown and paper-thin. His hair was matted, clumped with dried leaves and bird feathers. And he stunk. Pheap shrieked in horror when he examined her fingers.

"Spit on her fingers and wrap them in moss," he rasped. "She will be fine."

Hearing her thin, helpless cries, I wished we could leave that horrible place and join our ancestors.

Chapter Fourteen

Rice Harvest

The stream was a cracked mud cake. Our thirst led us farther and farther from camp, chasing the ponds as they disappeared. Throats dry, bellies swollen, eyes glazed, we shuffled to work in the fields and home again. We had barely enough strength to repair the dikes in preparation for the rainy season, but if we didn't work, we'd be kicked out of the cafeteria line or killed.

Finally, the golden stalks were ready to harvest. No matter how decrepit or ill, we worked; the promise of heaping bowls of sticky rice spurred us on.

My job was threshing the rice. The thump of rice stalks slapping the threshing board became my favorite sound. Watching the brown kernels tumble into the basket, I couldn't stop myself: I sneaked a few when no one was looking and sucked on them.

Ceremonies were forbidden by *Angka*. Still, the first meal after the harvest felt like a feast. The leaders allowed us to eat as much rice as we wanted. We shared the ripened pumpkins from our garden. Others added corn, cucumbers, and squash. Our bowls overflowed with rice and vegetables. Pheap, Saveun, and I went back for three helpings!

On this occasion, *Angka*'s rules only applied to us. We could hear the soldiers in their houses, singing and carousing, having a celebration of their own.

With no guards around, a few of the more daring quietly gave thanks to Buddha. Others sang traditional festival songs and danced. Luon, my cousins, and I were content to sit and watch, our bellies stuffed for the first time since we had left the farm.

Chapter Fifteen
On My Own

Early one morning, three soldiers I'd never seen before came to our hut. They ordered me to gather my things and come with them.

Saveun started to cry. Luon clamped her hand over the girl's mouth. "You know what happens to those who cry."

I thought of Somaly, a woman who had worked in the cafeteria. The harvest had been too late to save her child. All day she sat, clutching the dead boy's body. Her mournful cries filled the air until a soldier hit her.

"Your bawling is hurting my ears!" he screamed. "If you're that sad to lose your son, you can join him." He dragged Somaly into the woods. Then we heard the gunshot. We knew she wouldn't be back.

Stifling my sorrow, I wrapped my only change of clothes in my *krama* and followed the soldiers.

A group of about fifty boys and girls were already in front of the cafeteria. Some were from our camp; the rest I'd never seen before.

"You have been chosen by *Angka* for the honor of planting a new rice field," announced one of the soldiers. "Come with us."

Balancing our rice bowls on our heads, we trailed behind the soldiers as they marched away from camp. I didn't know where I was going or if I'd ever see my family again. I knew that Luon, Pheap, and Saveun were watching me, but I was too afraid even to turn my head for one last look.

Long after the sun had set, we arrived at our new camp, Srai Bun Jul. Though its name meant Four Row Rice Paddy, there were few remnants of the thriving farm it once had been. We stopped at a cluster of dilapidated shacks.

"Here is where you will live until your dormitories are finished," said the soldiers.

The shacks stunk of mildew and decay. Weeds and vines seemed to be the only things holding the walls together. We had to clear debris from the rotting floor before we could sleep.

Cricket, cicada, and locust calls melded with the night breathing of bodies crammed into the tiny shelter. Wrapping my *krama* around me, I looked up through the half-roof. The moon shone so brightly that it made the night look like day. I wondered if the moon was as bright in Vietnam. For the first time, I believed I'd never see my mother again. I cried until I had no more tears.

The next morning we were herded together. More children than I had ever seen in my life—two hundred fifty, maybe three hundred—shivered in the pre-dawn cold.

The soldiers separated the boys from the girls, and then they divided the boys into groups of ten. Each group had a leader. The leader of my group was a boy of about sixteen with a big head and ears that stuck out. We called him Pumpkin Head.

Old people were brought to the camp to build dormitories, which were simply thatched bamboo shelters on stilts with no walls, only bamboo poles holding up a hay roof. The girls lived in one, the boys in another; in between was a kitchen. The Khmer Rouge soldiers lived in separate houses with walls, windows, and their own kitchen.

My group was assigned to one part of the dormitory with just enough room to spread our mats on the floor. Bin, the boy next to me, hung his extra shirt between our mats like a curtain.

"I need a new shirt," said another boy, pulling it down.

Bin grabbed it back. "That's my shirt!"

Their arguing attracted Pumpkin Head's attention. He tore the shirt from Bin's hand. "Everything belongs to everyone," he said, handing the shirt to the other boy.

Bin eyed my extra pants and shirt. Not wanting to lose them, I lay down and tucked them under my head.

Chapter Sixteen
Life in the Camp

Each day in the camp began the same way. Before daybreak, someone banged a piece of metal against a hubcap to wake us. This was the signal to get up and get dressed. Most mornings we were so exhausted that we could barely pull ourselves off the floor.

Clang, clang! We dragged ourselves out of the dormitory and lined up. We stood with our left hand on the shoulder of the person in front of us. When each row was straight, the camp leader checked to see if we were all there. His face was pocked with scars, and he didn't walk right. He was called Crooked.

If a boy was missing, Crooked made us stand there until he was found. Usually the missing person would be relieving himself or had overslept. Sometimes, a boy ran away. Then Crooked would limp up and down the rows.

"*Angka* has eyes like pineapples!" he screamed. "*Angka* sees everything. The only place there is no *Angka* is underground. When we find the miserable worm, he can have his wish."

We'd stand there all day, the sun beating down on our heads, while soldiers searched for the boy.

On the third clang, we marched to work in a cornfield five or six kilometers away. Trees surrounded the field, with some cleared patches in between. It looked like it had once been farmed.

"Before the foreign invaders took over, Kampuchea was a great nation," Crooked had told us, banging his stick on the table. "At the divine temple of Angkor, our ancestors built an empire of plenty. They didn't just harvest one measly rice crop a year; they grew rice all year round. Now that the foreigners have been expelled, it is time to return to our former greatness. *Angka* deserves not just one, but two or three rice crops a year. That is why you are here."

To make new rice paddies for *Angka*, we lined up across a clearing, an arm's length apart. Using long, curved knives called *parangs*, we walked the length of the field, hacking away the tall grasses.

The smallest boy in my group, Phally, had pale skin and light eyes. From the way he spoke, I knew that he was from a rich family and had gone to school. Of all the boys in my group, he was the most pleasant. I liked to work next to him.

Because he was so small, Phally had a hard time cutting grass. The *parang* was heavy, and he tired easily, often falling behind everyone else. When I was beside him, I made wide, sweeping slices with my *parang*, clearing some of his strip along with mine. While Pumpkin Head praised me for my hard work, Phally thanked me with his eyes.

One time Phally lagged far behind. Pumpkin Head and another group leader started kicking and punching him.

"No good, lazy son of a Chinese mother!" they chided him. "Move faster! Work harder!"

Phally started to cry. The leaders kept yelling insults and slapping him. The louder he cried, the harder they hit. Because I had a narrow nose and lighter skin too, I was afraid they would turn on me next. I tried not to listen to Phally's screams. I cut faster so I wouldn't fall behind the others.

From then on, I avoided Phally. I rubbed dirt on my face, my hair, and my body. I took off my shirt and never covered my head so that the sun would burn me. I wanted to be as dark as the pure Khmers.

• • •

Every day, from dawn to dusk, we worked. On our only break, we followed our leader back to camp and lined up for a ration of rice soup mixed with vegetables and pieces of banana trunk—the same slop we used to feed the pigs.

We gulped our rations. We had to get back to work quickly, or we'd be punished. One day was like the next; only the jobs changed.

Picking wild potatoes was a job that no one liked. The potatoes grew inside a thorny bush. We had to be very careful picking them, or the thorns would cut deep gashes in our skin. When Ren, a new boy in our group, was sent to pick potatoes, he refused.

"Go to work!" said Pumpkin Head, hitting Ren's legs with a stick.

"I don't have shoes," whined Ren. "The thorns will cut my feet. You have shoes. Why don't you go?"

"You can have mine," said Pumpkin Head, removing his shoes.

Incredulous, Ren reached out his hand. Pumpkin Head hit him with the shoe. We laughed. He hit him again. He was still hitting him when we left camp. I didn't know why we were laughing, but we couldn't stop.

That night, we were roused from our sleep and called to a meeting. Ren, bruised and bloody, was dragged into the clearing.

"See this worthless dog?" said Crooked, kicking Ren over onto his back. "He refused to pick potatoes. He thinks he's better than everyone. Since he won't pick the potatoes, maybe he'd like to be a potato."

A group leader came forward. "I don't think we should kill him. Look how dark his skin is. He's a true Khmer, not tainted by foreign blood."

Pumpkin Head agreed. "I beat sense into him," he said proudly.

While the camp leaders continued their debate over Ren's fate, the rest of us struggled to stay awake, too tired to care what happened.

•   •   •

I was never too tired to climb the giant tamarind tree. Because I was the best climber in camp, the cafeteria people often asked me to pick its pods. In return, they'd give me a drink of the juice they made from the seeds.

I would have climbed the tree even if they hadn't rewarded me. When I reached the top, I stretched myself over the branches and stared up at the sky. For a brief moment, the camp disappeared, and I was back on the farm in Small Bor. Luon was washing clothes in the stream. Pheap and Saveun were playing with their cornstalk dolls. As usual, shellfire from the far-off war peppered the evenness of our days. Each time we lit incense, we prayed for the war to end. How could we have known that when the acrid shellfire haze lifted, when the bombs were finally still, we'd be caught in a different battle—the battle to survive?

"Hey, boy!" an old woman called up to me, rousing me from my reverie. "Be careful. There's a grave under that tree, and the ghosts will get you."

Since the Pol Pots had abolished Buddhism, we weren't allowed to help our ancestors pass into another life. The ghosts of all the people that the Khmer Rouge had killed were wandering around, angry because they couldn't rest. To disturb one would bring bad luck. My family didn't need any more bad luck! I shimmied down the trunk.

The cook berated me when I returned to the kitchen empty-handed.

"I can't climb that tree," I explained. "A ghost lives there."

"There's no need to be afraid of the ghost. He's dead." The cook waved her knife at me. "Be afraid of me. I'm alive!"

They made me climb the tree many times after that, but I never daydreamed in its branches again.

•   •   •

"I wish Pumpkin Head hadn't made me give up my other shirt," Bin complained one evening, trying to mend his clothes with our group's only needle.

"You can have mine," I offered. "I don't wear it."

"I don't want yours," said Bin, his eyes fastened on one of the group leaders. "I want his."

Two days later, the leader's shirt was hanging between our mats.

"Take it down!" I whispered, sure he'd stolen it.

"Why should I?" asked Bin. "I won it from him."

The next time I saw him, Bin was wearing a new hat, then a pair of sandals and pants. I waited and watched. Bin was never questioned about his new clothes.

"How are you winning all these things?" I finally asked.

"Come with me when we get a break," he said. "I'll show you."

Several boys were already inside the old farm shack when we arrived.

"I swiped a dried fish," said one of the boys.

"Who wants this?" called another, waving a *krama*.

I saw Bin eyeing the bright red *krama*. "I do," he said, pushing his way to the front.

Everyone else stepped back, clearing a space. Bin threw his grass hat on the ground beside the fish and *krama*. The three boys faced one another in the center of the room. They slid their pants down around their knees and knelt on the ground. In unison, they stuck their butts in the air.

Nobody moved. We were all waiting, listening. *For what?* I wondered.

Bin was the first to fart.

"One! Two! Three!" The onlookers counted each eruption. The other two boys began passing gas. The watchers divided into groups, counting and rooting for their favorite farter.

I watched, mesmerized. How did they suck the air in and let it out again?

"Twenty-two, twenty-three...." Bin had farts left long after the others had collapsed.

On the way back to work, Bin, sporting his new red *krama*, shared a bit of the dried fish and promised to teach me how to fart.

Chapter Seventeen
I Have No Friends

The Khmer Rouge encouraged us to inform on each other. We were constantly asked if we knew anyone who was educated or had mixed nationalities. In the meetings, the leaders said we'd be helping if we told on each other because then the offenders could be re-educated to serve *Angka*. When they questioned me, I earnestly nodded my head. "My family are farmers," I said, no matter what they asked.

At Srai Bun Jul I was given more to eat than at Phnom Pong. Still, I was hungry. The group leaders received more rice and extra vegetables. I couldn't stop myself from staring at their heaping bowls. Pumpkin Head knew that I was watching. One day he brought his bowl and sat beside me under a pepper tree.

"You can have more to eat, too, *met*," he said, gnawing on a chicken wing. "All you have to do is tell me what the others are saying, and I'll make sure you get more to eat. I like you. I know you're not stupid like the others say you are. I'm your friend."

I kept my head bent and continued eating. *I have no friends. I have no friends,* I told myself over and over. *I have no friends.*

One boy in our group, called Phuoc, cried himself to sleep every night. I wished I could cry, too, but I had cried myself out on the first night. I squeezed my eyes closed. After many nights of hearing him cry, Pumpkin Head crept over to Phuoc's mat and sat down.

"Hush," he whispered, patting Phuoc on the back. "I am your friend. Tell me why you're crying. You'll feel better."

"I can't," Phuoc sniffled.

Pumpkin Head softened his voice until I could barely hear him, coaxing until Phuoc began to talk.

"I miss my family," Phuoc sobbed, "and my home. They took my father away. I'm afraid he's dead."

"What does your father do?" Pumpkin Head wheedled.

"He owns the biggest store in Phnom Penh," Phuoc answered.

"You must be very proud of him," said Pumpkin Head. Phuoc told how good his life had been—his large house full of servants, elaborate parties his parents held, his mother's set of silver chopsticks and gold dishes.

"At Tet, my parents let my brothers and me help decorate the Caynau Pole for the New Year's celebration. We hung lucky red paper inscriptions, colorful cock feathers, and offerings for the good spirits on the pole and stood it in front of our house."

It felt good and hurt at the same time to listen to Phuoc reminisce. Tet was the biggest Vietnamese holiday of them all. Everyone in my family would come together for the week of festivities. But I willed Phuoc to stop talking. Didn't he realize that the Pol Pots were getting rid of everyone who was not Khmer? Didn't he understand how dangerous his memories were?

"Did your family give you new clothes and special cakes and candies, too?" asked Pumpkin Head.

"Oh, yes," said Phuoc. "And a shiny red envelope full of money."

Be quiet! I screamed in my head, but Phuoc was lost in his memories.

Phuoc was taken from the field the next day. The day after that, Pumpkin Head was wearing Phuoc's sandals.

· · ·

My malaria came back. This time it was accompanied by a ringing in my ears. I attempted to clear the passages by poking them with sticks. One moment I was burning hot, the next shivering. I was nauseated and barely able to walk.

"No work, no food," Pumpkin Head said.

So every day I dragged myself to the field, shaky and dizzy. Sometimes I'd ask a boy to pinch me. Little pinches on my back and chest made me feel better for a short while.

One morning, when the hubcap sounded the wake-up call, Bin had four heads. Clang, clang, clang! The sound reverberated throughout my body. I couldn't feel my feet. I couldn't pull myself off my mat.

Splash! A pail of warm liquid hit my face. Gasping, I rolled to my side. I was soaked with urine.

"You have no race!" shouted Pumpkin Head, jerking me to my feet. To say that I had no race—no heritage, no family honor—was the worst insult of all. Without letting me wash the burning waste from my eyes, Pumpkin Head pushed me out of the dormitory.

My group had been assigned to cut bamboo. While we worked, Pumpkin Head and a couple of other leaders sat under a tree. "Hurry up, piss head!" they called, laughing and waving their guns at me.

I widened my stance and bent my knees to steady myself, hacking at the stalks as fast as I could. I didn't want any more trouble. My *parang* hit Ren. It didn't cut him, but he cried out anyway.

"You hurt him!" screamed Pumpkin Head. "I'm going to send you to *Angka*!"

I sank to my knees. "I didn't mean to do it," I cried. "The knife slipped. I'll be more careful."

Pumpkin Head wouldn't listen. "You'll go to *Angka* for this! Just wait till tonight."

Luckily for me, the meeting that night was canceled. But Pumpkin Head devised a punishment of his own. "Since you can't be trusted not to cut someone with your *parang*, you will clear the grasses while everyone else sleeps," he informed me

Until then, by staying close to the group and not going out in the dark alone, I'd been able to hide the fact that I had night blindness. But that night there was not even a sliver of a moon to show me the difference between the jungle and the cleared field. I groped around blindly, swinging the *parang*, hoping to cut the grasses, scared all the time of what punishment Pumpkin Head would inflict on me if I didn't do a good job.

Whack! A blow to my shoulder knocked me to the ground.

"You've been wasting time!" shouted Pumpkin Head. "Anyone else would've had this skinny strip of grass cleared hours ago. You're a disgrace to *Angka*!"

"Please, please," I begged. "I can't see!"

"I'm sick of your excuses!" he screamed. "*Angka* almost lost a worker because of your carelessness, and now you take my time for nothing!"

"I tried to clear the grass," I explained, "but I can't see in the dark."

Pumpkin Head kept hitting, and I kept pleading until suddenly he stopped. "I'm being too hard on you," he said.

Though puzzled, I was grateful for his abrupt change of attitude. Meekly, I let him lead me away.

"You need to rest somewhere nice and quiet," he said soothingly. "Then maybe your sight will return." He eased me onto the ground. "Sleep here tonight. You'll feel better in the morning."

When I awoke in the morning and looked around, my blood froze. The nice, quiet bed that Pumpkin Head had chosen for me was on a grave. I had spent the night in a cemetery.

Pumpkin Head knew I'd told the truth about not being able to see at night, but he wasn't through with me. He made me work alone, carrying buckets of dirt from the jungle and dumping them at the edge of the field. Though this was meant as a punishment, I liked it. It gave me time to forage for food.

On one side, the field bordered a grove of fruit trees. We were forbidden to go there. But I would pass by the grove while carrying loads of dirt. I saw mangoes, bananas, and milkfruit hanging, ripe and heavy, from the trees. The fruit almost drove me crazy. I sneaked into the grove. I was about to pick a mango when I saw the wires. They were everywhere. Grenades and bombs were wired to the trees. Slowly, I backed away. Scanning the ground for fallen fruit, I saw that mines had been buried all around the area. Carefully, I tiptoed away.

Chapter Eighteen
The Lovers

They didn't hear or see me. I would have startled them if they hadn't been whispering—Bin and a girl, wrapped in each other's arms. I knew I should turn away, but my feet were rooted to the spot, my eyes glued to the lovers. I finally understood Bin's frequent disappearances, the half-smile on his lips no matter how hard Pumpkin Head worked him, and his sudden interest in his appearance.

I was scared for Bin and the girl. If I'd found them, how long would it be before someone else did? The leaders' words rang in my head: "Boys and girls should not be wasting time talking to each other. You can't work hard for *Angka* if you don't have a pure mind and body. If you have extra time, you must spend it working for *Angka*." Meeting after meeting, they'd warned us to stay away from girls.

My awareness of Bin's secret had somehow made me feel a party to it. I was obsessed with his whereabouts, as if by knowing where he was, I could protect him.

But I couldn't.

"I have something to report," announced Phally at a meeting. "Two of our comrades have not been good Khmers."

I knew without having to look that Phally was pointing to Bin and the girl.

"They've been meeting secretly," Phally continued, "lying together in the forest. They sneak away from the dormitories at night. During the day, they sneak away from the field to talk about love, leaving the rest of us to do their work."

While Crooked congratulated Phally for being a good Khmer, Bin and the girl were dragged to the front. Declaring that the girl had enticed Bin with her looks, Crooked pulled up tufts of her hair and hacked them off with his knife. Then he threw her to the ground while he railed at Bin for his weakness. "We work to grow food that you eat. You repay us by betraying *Angka*'s laws. You think only of yourself."

Soldiers tied Bin and the girl back to back. I hugged my knees while the leaders took turns beating them. When they fainted from pain, they were revived and beaten some more.

Finally, we were allowed to leave. I curled up on my mat, turning my back on the empty place beside me.

Chapter Nineteen
The Rainy Season

If I thought that life was as bad as it could get, I was wrong. By the end of the dry season, our only food was a half can of water with a few grains of rice in it. Animals and bugs had disappeared with the streams. We chased the ponds, walking two hours or more to fill our bowls with brackish, muddy water. We chewed leaves to relieve our thirst and worked with pebbles under our tongues so our mouths wouldn't be so dry. The air, heavy with moisture, pushed down on me, making it hard to lift my limbs. I wished I could squeeze the water out of the sky.

The day the rain came, the entire camp ran outside, laughing and jumping. Even leaders lifted their faces to the falling water. People scurried about setting pots under the edges of roofs to catch the precious runoff.

Rivers overflowed and flooded the entire region. My group was sent to dig canals to contain the rising water. We filled baskets with mud, dumping them on the sides to build a wall. No sooner would we complete a section than the rain-soaked dirt would give way, and the wall would slide back into the ditch.

Ticks were the worst part about digging the canals. The place was infested with them. By the hundreds, they attached themselves to our bodies, especially between our legs. They were so tiny that we had to leave them, knowing they were sucking our blood, until they were big enough to pick off.

The rain fell, the water rose, and we dug, resting as often as Pumpkin Head would allow. The ringing in my ears from the malaria was gone, but my head still felt swollen—filled with greenish-yellow pus that dripped steadily out of my ears and onto my hair and shoulders.

During a break, I headed for a stand of trees. Out of the corner of my eye, I saw Pumpkin Head turn from the group of leaders and start toward me, waving his gun and shouting. I strained to make out his words. "Where do you think you're going?" he shouted.

"To get out of the rain."

"You don't have permission to leave," he said.

Turning back, I slipped. Part of the hill slid down with me. In my struggle to free myself from the mud, I uncovered a body. I was sitting on it. All around me were parts of bodies reaching out from their shallow graves.

Choking down the bile that filled my throat, I hurried back to work.

Chapter Twenty
Tired and Hungry

A tall, spindly-legged egret pulled in its wings and landed with a swish on the black, swollen earth just inside the clearing. I held my breath, watching it inch toward the kernels of rice. The egret cocked its head as if it were listening to the other, wiser egrets cautioning it from the trees. Ruffling its feathers, it spread its wings and was gone.

Leaving my hiding place behind a sugar palm, I carefully picked up every kernel of rice from the ground.

The birds in the trees mocked me. They were too smart to let themselves be caught for a few kernels of rice. Like the rats and lizards, they had taken to hiding deeper in the jungle, too greedy for life to be caught in my traps.

I stuffed the handful of rice—dirt and all—into my mouth. *Better a little rice than nothing,* I thought.

The birds and the steady plop, plop, plop of moisture dripping from the stalks of the bamboo and the wide, flat leaves of the palm and banana trees were all I could hear as I picked my way back through the thicket. I knew that the boys in my group were resting just beyond the jungle, but I heard no sound from them. After more than two years of rising before the sun, trudging through the vine-tangled jungle to the rice paddies, bending and digging, planting, and carrying buckets of water in the dry season and rocks and dirt in the wet—years of being scared and tired and hungry—no one had the energy to talk or sing or laugh anymore.

Chapter Twenty-One
New Year

Grinding gears brought us to attention. We jumped up from our mats. Wide-eyed, we watched the driver of the first of a convoy of army supply trucks enter Khmer Rouge headquarters.

"The trucks are full of guns!"

"Or soldiers!"

"They've come to take us away!"

"This happened at my other camp," someone said. "The Vietnamese were told to gather their belongings and get in the trucks. The leaders said they were going back to Vietnam. It was a lie. They were all killed." My mind raced with thoughts of escape. *Where could I go? What could I do?* I took hold of myself. *No one knows I'm part Vietnamese.* I hadn't told anyone about my heritage. I examined my arms and legs. They were as brown as a pure Khmer's. My clothes were the same, my hair, too. By the time the driver got out, I'd convinced myself that I had nothing to worry about. I also knew that no matter what, I wasn't going to get in one of those trucks.

When the driver threw back the canvas sides, I saw that we'd been worrying for nothing. Wooden crates with

Chinese writing on them filled one of the trucks. Others were full of sacks of rice and canned food.

After the trucks left, a meeting was called.

"Through the goodness of *Angka*, you will all receive new clothes for your backs and food for your stomachs," said Crooked.

Each of us was given a new shirt and trousers. Pumpkin Head was given a real treasure: a bar of soap! That afternoon, we stood in the rain, laughing and splashing and sharing the bar of soap.

At supper, in our new clothes, we feasted on bowls of sticky rice chock full of hot peppers, vegetables, canned pineapple, and a strange pale yellow paste that I'd never tasted before—applesauce.

"Lazy Lon Nols!" Crooked's angry voice interrupted our meal. "You think you get food for nothing? Get up and go to work!"

Our bellies full for the first time in many months, we didn't mind the work. Pumpkin Head and the other leaders scurried about. I'd never seen them so agitated, but their frantic behavior didn't dampen our spirits. When Ren started singing work songs, everyone joined in:

> Clear the jungle.
> Plant the crop for *Angka*.
> We work in a hurry
> So *Angka* will have strength from the food
> And get energy to fight Lon Nol.

About the third time through, Ren changed the words:

Chop the firewood.
Hull the rice.
We work in a hurry
So Pumpkin Head and Crooked will be happy
And give us food to eat.

Midway through the verse, Pumpkin Head appeared, and the singing stopped.

"Don't stop. The singing is good," he said, sounding unusually solicitous and friendly.

"Are the cuts on your arms healing?" he asked a boy who had fallen into a patch of wild potatoes.

We all knew that this boy's cuts weren't getting better. In spite of the mudpacks he'd put on them, the angry red slashes oozed pus and hurt so badly that he cried every day.

"The trucks brought medicine," said Pumpkin Head, inspecting the wounds. "Go to headquarters and get some." He motioned to another boy. "Go with him. You haven't been able to work for two days. Any of the rest of you who need medicine can go, too."

The gashes on my legs from chopping bamboo throbbed. I wanted to join the others, but I remembered Luon's cautiousness. *I'll wait and see if they get better,* I thought. When the boys who had gone to get medicine were missing from roll call the next morning, I was glad I'd waited.

Before long, we discovered why Crooked had given us food and new clothes and made us clean everything so thoroughly, and why all the sick children had vanished. The leaders were getting ready for an inspection.

That afternoon, the inspectors arrived. From the way Crooked and the others fawned over the three men, we knew they were from *Angka*.

We kept our eyes lowered as the men marched down the columns, scrutinizing us. Crooked bustled along behind them, pointing out how hard we worked and bragging about the rice crop.

One of the men climbed onto the back of the jeep. "Today is the glorious second anniversary of the rebirth of Kampuchea," he announced. "It is a time for joy and celebration. You see what we have accomplished now that the foreigners have been driven from our homeland. You have new clothes. Your stomachs are full. The rice fields are multiplying, and we will have more rice than ever before. Hard work has made us prosper."

This is why the trucks had come with clothes and food, I thought. *How powerful and omniscient is* Angka *if Crooked and the other leaders can fool these men into believing that we're thriving?*

"As a reward for your hard work and to celebrate the New Year," the man in the jeep continued, "*Angka* is declaring a holiday. For three days there will be no work. Visit your families, rest, and rejoice!"

Pumpkin Head told us that we could each pick a stalk of bananas. Safe from watchful eyes, I let out my feelings of joy. I don't know where the energy came from. I was so excited that I chopped down the biggest bunch I could find to take to Luon and my cousins.

I didn't want Luon to know how bad things were. I tried to make myself look as good as possible. I scrubbed my teeth with a twig until my gums bled, and I cut my long, scraggly hair.

Afraid that the soldiers would stop me on the way to Phnom Pong, I boiled my new clothes with tree root to make them black. I wanted them to be as black as a leader's uniform. I thought that if I looked like the Khmer Rouge, they'd leave me alone. I boiled the clothes for hours. When it was time to leave, I stepped into the trousers, but they fell to shreds! So did my new shirt! I had cooked them too long.

Chapter Twenty-Two
Luon Is Sick

Dressed in my old rags, bananas slung over my shoulder, I arrived at Phnom Pong. Luon and the girls could only stare, their faces cavernous, their eyes yellow and glazed. Their legs, big as tree trunks, hurt so badly that they could barely walk. Pheap, who had always flitted about, now sat in a corner, folded into a ball. She didn't seem to recognize me, but when I tried to leave, wouldn't let me go. She slept clutching my fingers.

Sadly, I recalled the glorious picture that Mir Ton had painted of Kampuchea's future the morning he'd left the farm. *I hope Mir Ton is dead,* I thought, *so he never has to know what the Khmer Rouge have done to us!*

I couldn't bear to think of Luon and the girls lying in filth, unprotected below the ragged palm roof. I started fixing the hut. Several times I stopped working long enough to coax them into eating a few bites of mashed banana. I carried Pheap and Saveun to the stream and bathed them. Luon was too proud to let me carry her, so I sponged her face, arms, and legs with damp moss. My need to provide for them overcame my exhaustion. Late that night I sneaked into the jungle. I collected edible roots, tubers, and strips of bark and buried them below Saveun's mat before finally allowing myself to rest.

I awoke with a start. Luon was leaning over me. She had dragged herself across the floor, and she was motioning for me to follow. We crawled past my sleeping cousins and out of the hut. The crazed look in Luon's eyes as she clawed at the ground scared me. She uncovered a handful of pale melons hidden beneath the leaves.

"Take good care of these. No one knows I'm growing them. If they find out, they'll steal them. They steal everything!" Luon hissed, clenching her broken teeth. "They stole our clothes. They stole Pheap's mat. They even stole our rice pot! What more can they do to us? These Khmer Rouge! These 'saviors'! They made us leave our home, forget our language and customs. They forced us to hide our ancestors and disgrace ourselves. They make us afraid because our skin is not dark, our eyes are not Khmer, our ways are not ignorant. They want us to be animals like they are."

"Shhh," I said. "Someone might hear you."

"I'm sick, Mok. I'm going to die."

A knot swelled in my chest. "Don't say that!"

"Look at me," she said. "Look at my legs, my stomach. I can't work the fields. They've cut my rations. I'm going to die like all the others. They're going to kill me like they killed my husband."

"Don't talk that way," I admonished. "Mir Ton is alive."

Luon shook her head. "I've known he was dead ever since we saw the piles of soldiers' bodies on the road. But I still have the jewels." Luon pushed the hem of her tunic against my palm. "Feel them? They are our secret."

After reassuring Luon—and myself, too—that the jewels were valuable, I convinced her to let me help her inside.

When the New Year's holiday was over, I left Phnom Pong in despair, not knowing if I'd ever see Luon, Pheap, or Saveun again.

Chapter Twenty-Three
The Rat Bite

The truckloads of food at Srai Bun Jul disappeared with the inspectors. Hunger was once again my constant companion. I ate anything I could find to take away the pain in my stomach—red ants, centipedes, termites, grubs, or a rat if I could catch one. One night, the pain was so bad that I couldn't sleep. I tied splinters of bamboo with blades of grass to make a rat trap.

In the morning, on my way to the field, I set the trap. To hold it in place, I tied the trap to a stick and pounded the stick into the ground. Baiting it with the only piece of meat I'd found floating in my soup, I beseeched Buddha to bring a rat to my trap.

He did—a big, fat, brown one! As I got closer, the rat struggled to free itself, and the trap broke loose from the stick I had set in the ground. Afraid I'd lose the rat, I grabbed the trap. The rat snapped at me, its sharp teeth sinking into the flesh between my fingers. I screamed and tried to shake it loose. When that didn't work, I hit it with a rock. The rat squealed and let go of my hand. The trap shattered when it hit the ground. I watched my meal disappear into the underbrush.

Almost immediately the bite began to swell. It hurt so much that I could hardly use my hand to do my work.

"Get to work, you stupid, lazy boy, or you won't get any food!" Pumpkin Head ordered.

"I'm working as hard as I can," I explained, showing him the bloody, jagged rat bite.

He pushed my hand aside. "You get only a half portion of rice today."

Each day the wound grew worse. I was afraid to show it to anyone because I'd lose my rice portion again. Finally, I couldn't stand it any longer. My hand was swollen to three times its normal size, and red streaks radiated from the wound. I showed it to an old woman who knew how to make medicine from plants.

The old woman clicked her tongue. "It's full of poison," she said. "If you don't take care of it, you'll lose your hand." From the folds of her *krama*, she took out some leaves. "Boil these in urine, and soak the bite until all the red lines are gone."

Chapter Twenty-Four
The Island

The infected rat bite didn't improve. The red lines traveled up my arm and across my chest and neck. My head, fiery hot, felt like a giant balloon stretched tight with pain. I shook uncontrollably. I couldn't work anymore.

"Why waste food on him?" asked Crooked. "He's going to die anyway."

Splotches of red, purple, green, and bright gold popped and swirled before my eyes. I tried to focus on the colors. They changed into candied fruit, ice cream, fried bananas, spicy pork. I could smell the food. I could taste it. The food pictures and the pain drove me crazy.

I dreamed of the island in the middle of one of the rice paddies. It wasn't much of an island—just a mound of earth with a tree growing in the center. Whenever Pumpkin Head let us rest, we'd climb out of the knee-deep water and crowd onto it. When we first went there, the island was alive with animals and bugs. I never left without something tucked into my pant leg to eat later.

In my dream, I was sitting under the tree, its flowered branches shading me, cooling the fire in my body. Paddy crabs and shrimp crawled all over me.

When I awoke, my stomach pulled me to the island. I staggered through camp to the rice paddy, clawing through the dirt. When I got to the island, I leaned against the tree, listening to the cicadas.

Suddenly, the cicadas stopped singing. When they didn't start again, I listened. I could hear voices. Soldiers! They were marching in my direction!

Acting on instinct, I climbed into the tree to hide. I could hear the soldiers coming through the paddy. They tossed their loads on the ground and lounged under the tree not ten feet below me. They joked and ate.

Like a monkey, I clung to the branch, using all the strength I had just to hold on. My head throbbed; the colors whirled. I shut my eyes, trying to force them away, but the red, purple, and bright gold spots flashed and swirled and blurred.

Chapter Twenty-Five
The Death Wagon

The rickety old bus jerked to a halt in front of the marketplace. I struggled to open my eyes.

"Are we there already, Luon?" I asked.

Where was she? Where were the pigs and baskets of fruit? I blinked, trying to focus.

I wasn't on the town bus; I was in the back of a truck full of bamboo. I could hear voices. The words were drowned out by the sound of the motor and the buzzing in my head.

"They've stopped to move some logs blocking the road," said a voice in my ear.

I strained to sit up.

"Aiyiiii!" the man screamed. "Watch my leg!" Inches from my hand was a stump of what had been a leg, wrapped in a dirty, blood-soaked rag.

"Where are they taking us?" I asked.

"To Battambang, to the hospital." The man was probably no older than Mir Ton, but he looked like he was already dead. His face, shiny with sweat, was drawn into a grimace. I knew that the stump was as painful as it looked. "We're on the death wagon," he said.

"But I'm not dead," I protested.

"You soon will be. We all will, if we're lucky," he said. "They only take you to the hospital when you can't work anymore, and they think you're going to die. Have you ever known anyone who came back from the hospital?"

In my mind, I saw Luon clutching Comrade Muy's leg, begging him to let me stay with her instead of sending me to the hospital. Slipping in and out of consciousness, I dreamed that I'd wandered into Comrade Muy's house, drawn by the smell of vegetables and fish cooking. Comrade Muy and his children were eating. There was a bottle of soy sauce beside the cooking pot. It had been so long since I'd seen a bottle of soy sauce. I could hear the children and Comrade Muy's wife screaming at me as I lifted it to my lips. Comrade Muy smacked the bottle from my hand.

He's going to kill me, I thought, staring at his hand resting on his gun.

"I'm so sick," I said. "Please don't kill me! I'm sorry." Comrade Muy took pity on me. He crushed a *gor* tree leaf in water and told me to drink it. I choked it down, feeling like I was eating a whole tree.

The next day, when Comrade Muy came to check on me, I was still feverish. "This boy needs to go to the hospital," he said, lifting me over his shoulder.

"Please don't send him there," begged Luon. "No one comes back from the hospital. I'll take care of him. He'll get better."

In my mind, Luon was still pleading when the truck started up and I was slammed against the side.

A woman groaned, her anguished cry echoed by others. For the first time, I noticed several bodies piled on top of the bamboo. The bamboo rocked and rolled with the motion of the truck. The one-legged man was still talking. Letting his words wash over me, I pressed myself against the side of the vehicle and closed my eyes again.

Chapter Twenty-Six
The "Die Place"

Two men threw me on the hospital floor and left me. The stench was so bad that I gagged and heaved. There wasn't anything in my stomach, but I couldn't stop. I crawled over to the wall and propped myself against it. The corridor was filled with people crying and moaning. Droning flies feasted on their mutilated and decaying bodies. Too weak to shoo them away, I was defenseless as they attacked my ears and eyes and invaded my nostrils. I closed my eyes and mouth to keep them out.

This section of the hospital was called the "die place." The floor was slimy with urine and feces since most of the patients, too weak to crawl to the bathroom, had soiled themselves and lay soaking in waste. An occasional breeze drifted through the tiny bathroom window, but it wasn't enough to alleviate the stench and the stifling heat.

The bathroom, like everything else in the once-modern hospital, had been left by the Khmer Rouge to deteriorate. Tiled in blue, the one and only toilet was a raised platform with a hole in the center. Though it was equipped with a tank and a pull-chain flusher, it had long since broken and overflowed with excrement. The waste putrefied until a worker happened by to bail it out. Since there was no toilet paper, people wiped themselves on the corners of walls. Maggots thrived on the feces and bloodstained surfaces.

Once a day a worker filled a bowl with watery soup and set it on my head in an attempt to keep it out of the filth. I knew it was there, but despite the grinding in my stomach, I was too weak to reach up and get it.

All around me, people were dying. I wanted to die, too. I lay in a stupor while hospital workers pushed me aside to remove bodies, and diarrhea-plagued patients stumbled over me on the way to the bathroom.

Srai Bun Jul had taught me to be invisible. When hospital workers came by, I practiced what I'd learned. No matter how much my head ached or my purple, bulbous legs and feet throbbed, I remained silent. I concentrated on the walls, tracing the cracks between the concrete blocks. Since I wasn't screaming or crying or bleeding, they didn't bother with me. Occasionally someone roused me with a kick. A groan was all they needed to let them know it was not time to throw me away.

One day my eye was forced open. "This one's almost gone."

Voices mingled in the space above me. "Give him a shot."

"It's just coconut milk."

"He doesn't know that. Maybe the shot will help."

"If we're lucky, it'll kill him, and we'll have one less to take care of."

My pants were pulled down. I tried to struggle away. A knee pressed into my back. My face was smashed into the clammy floor. A stab of pain shot through me as a needle was plunged into my thigh.

Chapter Twenty-Seven
Luon Comes

I lay in the top of the mango tree. The breeze tossed the branches, rocking me gently. Luon's scratchy, sweet singing drifted up from the yard. Far off, I could hear Pheap and Saveun playing. I sighed and opened my eyes. A shaft of light from the bathroom window illuminated the mildewed hospital ceiling. My spirits plunged. It was the dream again.

Cool hands touched my face. I turned my head. Luon's ghost was beside me. Chanting softly, she smoothed my face.

"I've been waiting for you, Luon," I said, lifting my arms to her. "I'm ready to die."

"You're not going to die," said Luon's ghost.

"But I want to be with you." I closed my eyes and reached toward her. "Please let me die."

"Wake up!" I felt a sharp twinge of pain where she pinched me. "It's me, Luon. I'm not dead!"

I rubbed my eyes. The vision didn't go away. It wasn't a ghost! Luon was alive! I was so happy to see her that my heart hurt.

"When I heard you were here, I pretended to be sick and begged for a hospital pass," she said. "They let me come only after I convinced them that I thought their phony doctors could cure me."

Luon untied the vines that were holding my clothes together. Tears slipped from her eyes when she peeled the rags away and saw the sores all over my body. Cradling my head, she plucked the lice from my hair and soothed me.

When it was time for her to leave, I hung onto her, begging her to stay.

"I've been assigned to a room on the other side of the hospital. I will come to see you whenever I can," she promised.

I lived for Luon's visits. Greedily devouring the rice balls, chicken, vegetables, and dried fruit she smuggled in, I didn't question where she got them or how. I began to regain my strength, and my vision cleared as the infected rat bite healed.

I was moved from the "die place" to a tiny room with a window. Four beds were crammed into it, two people to a bed. The man I shared a bed with was the biggest man I had ever seen. He took up all the space on the rusted, broken box springs. Grateful to be off the filthy floor, I squeezed myself into the space between his feet and the bottom of the bed.

The man smelled like he was rotting from the inside. I never knew his name or where he came from. The only time I was sure he was alive was when a worker came to clean. His head followed the constant swish, swish, swish of her broom against the cement floor.

A short time later, the man was carried away. I heard his hysterical screams and knew that the "doctors" were operating on him. Since the Khmer Rouge had killed or imprisoned the real doctors and nurses and had destroyed modern medicines, folk remedies were all that was left to treat the sick. When people had an infection in their arms or legs, they were given teas, herb pellets, and poultices to treat it. If those didn't work, the infected appendage was chopped off.

When the man was brought back, his arm was missing. It would be added to the mound of amputated body parts growing behind the hospital.

Chapter Twenty-Eight
Veun to the Rescue

"I've found you!" Luon squeezed between the beds. "When you weren't in the corridor, I was scared something bad had happened."

"They think I'm going to live, so they moved me," I told her. She smiled. Although her teeth were broken, her smile was the same one I remembered. Her face was round again.

"You've changed," I said, seeing her clearly for the first time. "When I left you at New Year's, you were sick. I thought you were going to die."

"I almost did," she said, "but a man saved us."

"What man?" I asked.

"Saveun met him first," Luon began. "We were starving. I couldn't walk. Since I couldn't work, they stopped feeding us. The food you hid kept us alive. Saveun was able to trap a few frogs. She took them from house to house and traded them for rice. That's how we met Veun. He's a pop singer from Siem Reap. He always traded with Saveun and often gave her something extra, like a piece of chicken or fish or even candy.

"I lay there day after day watching Saveun, sick herself, suffering to keep Pheap and me alive. I convinced myself that if I could stand up, the swelling would go down to my ankles, and I'd be able to work again. I must have been crazy. I pulled myself up and tried to walk.

"The next thing I knew, there was a bandage on my head, and I was lying on a mat covered in a clean *krama*. Veun was feeding me. He moved into our hut and has been taking care of us ever since. He has a good heart. He brings us rice and chicken and ducks. We bury them under the house, cooking only a little at a time so no one will be suspicious. Veun claims he gets the food from his parents, but he sneaks out at night when he thinks we're asleep and doesn't return until dawn. I think he's stealing from the Khmer Rouge, but I don't care. He saved our lives."

Luon's cheeks colored, and she dropped her eyes. "Veun is very proud that he's going to be a father."

Open-mouthed, I stared at Luon's bulging belly. I was so used to seeing people swollen from hunger that I laughed to think that Luon's stomach was swollen with new life.

On her next visit, Luon brought Veun and my cousins with her. They didn't have a pass, so they couldn't come into the hospital. Luon helped me over to the window. I couldn't take my eyes off Pheap and Saveun. They looked so different from the stony-faced skeletons I'd last seen.

Veun scooped Pheap up and started singing a love song. The girls giggled. It had been so long since I'd heard them happy. I never wanted them to stop laughing.

"What's going on here?" a hospital worker demanded. Immediately Veun switched to a Khmer Rouge song. The hospital worker listened for a moment, grunted, and left.

After that, Luon wasn't my only visitor. I never knew when Veun would show up. I'd hear his song and hurry to the window. With a wink and a smile, he'd toss up a treat.

Chapter Twenty-Nine
Going Fishing

The hospital wasn't far from the river. Everyone who could was sent there to bathe. Debris, bloated carcasses, garbage, machinery, and furniture littered the riverbed. The water was murky and foul-smelling, but it was alive with fish. Without a trap or line, however, I didn't know how to catch them.

"I'll show you," said Lundy, a boy bathing near me. "We'll split what we catch."

We waded into the river. Following Lundy's lead, I held my shirt under the water and waited for a fish to swim close. When I spotted one, I tried to scoop it into my shirt. At the end of the day, we'd caught six fish.

"I'm a better fisherman than you," said Lundy. "I get more." Laughing, he walked away, leaving me only the smallest fish.

As the weeks passed, I became a better fisherman. Lundy had taught me well. For every two fish I caught, I hid one, rolled into my pant leg. The more fish I caught, the shorter my pants got. Then, when Lundy teased me about being a lousy fisherman and took the best of the catch, I was the one who was laughing, my pants heavy with fish.

Once a day the "doctor" made his rounds. He was from a hill tribe. His skin was almost black, and his language consisted of grunts and gestures. With a basket full of homemade pills that looked like rabbit turds, he marched through the hospital, beads of sweat dripping from his bald head. He stuffed the slimy, green pellets down our throats with his thick fingers. Claiming that his syringe was filled with great medicine from *Angka*, he injected everyone, using the same needle over and over. He enjoyed giving shots.

The "doctor" kept rusty razor blades in his pocket. If he noticed a festering puncture wound from the dirty needle, he sliced it off, smiling his toothless grin while his victim screamed. Whenever I saw him coming, I hid.

One day, with my pants rolled almost to my crotch, I headed back to the hospital, dreaming of the fish I was going to eat. But I'd returned too early; the "doctor" was still making his rounds. I saw him and backed away. Too late! He saw me. He came toward me, waving the needle.

"No, no!" I pleaded. "I don't need the shot."

He pounced on me. With a crazed laugh, he drove the dirty needle into my stomach.

The place where the needle pierced my skin became swollen. I knew, after the rat bite, what would happen if I didn't have it taken care of. But I was scared to let anyone see it because they'd slice it off with a razor.

Luon went to a Kru Khmer. He told her to make a potion of wild tomatoes and a root from the buffalo trunk tree. Following his instructions, she rolled a piece of honeycomb inside a rice ball and burned it black. She boiled the rice ball with the potion and made me drink it. It tasted horrible.

Every day for about a month, just like Luon had done, I made the potion, cooking it over a fire behind the hospital. The old people sat around and watched and made fun of my root medicine. But the potion worked. The swelling went down, and the wound healed. Soon the old people wanted me to teach them how to make the medicine for themselves.

Chapter Thirty
We Move to the *Wat*

The hospital was suddenly silent. I peeked out of my room. Three soldiers I had never seen before stood in the corridor.

"The hospital's too crowded," they announced. "Anyone who can walk line up outside."

I scurried back to bed and pulled my *krama* over me. *Should I line up,* I agonized, *or should I pretend to be too sick to move?*

The soldiers made their way down the hall, pulling people from their beds. I heard a thud and an anguished cry.

"You can walk!" shouted a soldier. "Get up, or you'll be fertilizer for *Angka*!"

My decision was made. I joined the group amassed outside. While I waited to find out what the soldiers had planned for us, I thought about my family. Luon and the new baby girl had been sent back to Phnom Pong. Veun had promised to return for me. How would he know where I was?

Like cattle, we were herded, staggering and stumbling, through the ghost city of Battambang. The going was easier for me since I was stronger. Most of the others had been frightened out of their beds and were really too sick to be on their feet. Just ahead of me, a frail boy tumbled face down in the dirt.

"Get up!" shouted a soldier. "Keep moving!"

The boy struggled to raise himself. Zombie-like, the people moved past him. Even though the boy was covered in filth and reed-thin, something about him was familiar. I helped him to his feet.

Late in the afternoon, we stopped at a *wat* that was guarded by soldiers. The charred sign read "Battambang Main Temple." This fine old structure, which had once been home to more than a hundred monks, a place of peace and meditation, was now a place of death.

The soldiers pushed us inside. Everything in the temple had been demolished. Carved statues with severed heads, arms, and legs were strewn on the ground. Even the enormous Buddha in the center was riddled with bullet holes. The walls were gone. A fence had been built around the grounds. Already the area was crowded. Using whatever they could find, people had set up camp in the monks' gardens.

The boy I had helped was delirious. I cleared away some rubble, making a place for him to rest. While he slept, I studied his features. I knew him from somewhere, but I couldn't place him. Hunger and sickness had changed us all.

Not far from us, an old man fell to his knees before a decapitated Buddha and began to chant. Every few minutes, he'd throw back his head and scream. He made me uneasy. I pulled the boy to his feet and dragged him to a vacant corner of the yard behind what had been the kitchen.

The old man's high-pitched chanting penetrated the courtyard. Some soldiers broke away from a group that was gathered around a fire and approached the man. "Why are you praying, crazy old man?"

They took hold of his arms and legs. The old man never stopped chanting as they dragged him across the yard into the temple. "We'll fix you," they said, and they tied him to a cross made of bamboo. One of the soldiers pushed his gun into the old man's mouth. "I'm going to shoot you," he said.

The flow of garbled words continued as the old man moved his mouth around the gun barrel.

"He doesn't even know we're here," said another soldier. "He really is crazy."

They laughed and let the cross fall to the floor.

As soon as the soldiers left, people crowded around the crazy man. I thought they were going to untie him, but they didn't.

"Hurry up and die, crazy old man," they taunted. "We want your clothes."

The man's chanting and intermittent screams kept me awake all night. In the morning, people hovered over him. They couldn't wait until he was dead. They stripped him, leaving him tied to the cross. When he finally died, the soldiers threw him in the fire. I felt the heat of the flames in my bones. *I'll be in there someday,* I thought. Fed by an endless stream of bodies, the fire burned day and night.

The well in the *wat* was dry. The only water was in the river, three kilometers away. I'd bring back as much as I could carry in rusted gasoline cans and share it with the soldiers so they would let me come and go as I pleased.

On my way to the river, I passed by some abandoned buildings that Khmer Rouge families had moved into. I could smell the pigs, cows, and chickens they'd hidden. The thought of all that food nearly drove me crazy. I kept my eyes open, hoping to find a stray. Once I got lucky and found a dead chicken. It was diseased, but I ate it anyway.

A one-eyed man who lived in a hut by the trash ran errands for the soldiers. When the crazy man was dying, he had tried to keep people away. I knew that he was kind, so I brought him water, too. Sometimes he invited me into his hut. Rolling crushed *kai* in banana leaves, he'd smoke and tell stories about when he lived with the monks and guarded the offerings.

On one of my trips to the river, I saw some pig entrails floating in the water. I fished them out with my shirt and sneaked them back to the *wat* like a bundle of laundry. I took them to the one-eyed man.

"These intestines smell bad," he said. "They're rotten."

"If you cook them, won't they be okay to eat?" I asked.

"Maybe," he said. "But if the Pol Pots catch me cooking them, I'll be in trouble."

He finally agreed when I offered to share half with him. Pretending that we were making guava tree tea, we cooked the entrails in his tin can. We ate until our stomachs ached. That night our stomachs swelled with gas. We vomited up everything we'd eaten and more.

While we were starving, the Khmer Rouge had plenty. Late at night, I slipped out and dug through the trash for the soldiers' leavings. Sometimes I'd find overripe milkfruit, cucumbers that were just a little moldy, or leftover rice. This was a feast for the one-eyed man, the boy, and me.

I found an elephant trunk tree and cooked the potion Luon had taught me for the boy. Soon he was strong enough to help forage for food. Chasing crickets and toads with him felt familiar, but my mind had blocked my memories. Because the boy didn't talk, he couldn't help me remember.

Chapter Thirty-One
Grave Robbers

Lots of children lived in the *wat*. Most of them had formed little groups, helping one another survive. They tried to befriend me, too, but the camps had taught me to trust no one. Returning from a trip to the river, the boy and I were stopped by a boy called Nang. Everyone knew Nang because he was a troublemaker. Whenever anything was missing or a fight started, Nang was involved. I pretended not to notice him watching me, turning away whenever he passed. I wondered why he was interested in me.

"Where have you been?" asked Nang. I didn't answer. It was obvious from the gasoline cans we carried that we'd been to the river for water. "I know where you can find gold and jewels," he continued.

I stepped aside to pass him.

"Look at this." Nang pulled a jade pendant from his pocket.

"It's beautiful," I said, certain that it was stolen.

"There's lots more," he added.

"Why would you share them with me?" I asked. "Why don't you keep them for yourself?"

"Because I want you to teach me how to make the medicine that made him better," Nang said, pointing to the boy.

If Nang had asked me, I would have taught him how to make Luon's potion. He didn't need to bribe me. But the gold and jewels meant that we could have more food, and there was never enough of that.

Nang led us through the city, past the river to a grassy knoll. We stopped at a black iron fence surrounding a Chinese graveyard. Nang pushed open the gate. The creaking of its hinges set my teeth on edge.

Fresh mounds of dirt and splintered coffin boards showed where grave robbers had done their work. Pieces of skeleton, embroidered robes, and broken statues of dragons and tigers were strewn across the once-peaceful resting place. We followed Nang farther into the cemetery to a section where the graves were untouched, their shrines intact. Nang fell to his knees beside one of the graves. Carelessly tossing aside a porcelain pot of colorless plastic flowers, he began to dig.

I jumped as a piercing scream tore from the silent boy's throat. He charged past me and threw himself on Nang, pounding him with his fists. "Leave them alone! They didn't do anything! They just didn't want to leave home. Why did you kill them?"

It took all my strength to pull the boy off Nang. I tried to calm him, but he broke away and ran through the cemetery, picking up bones and pieces of clothing. Lovingly, he placed them back in the graves, all the while muttering, "I'll take care of you. I'll take care of you." He smoothed the soil and scooped sand back into incense bowls, sobbing ceaselessly.

"He's crazy!" Nang shouted, backing away. "You're both crazy. I'm getting out of here!"

I stayed with the boy. After a while he stopped crying. Slowly, he rose to his feet and began brushing the dirt off his legs and arms. "The soldiers in black ordered us to leave," the boy began. "Everyone in the village started packing, but my father and grandmother wouldn't leave our house. My mother begged my father. She cried, pleading with him to take us to my uncle's house. She was scared of the soldiers. My father just laughed at her. 'Silly woman,' he said, 'there's no reason to be scared. The Khmer Rouge are here to save us.'"

The boy's eyes never left the ground, his hands compulsively brushing the dirt. I knew that voice, and I recognized the story.

"My father was wrong!" The boy's anguished voice echoed through the silent cemetery. "We were sleeping when the soldiers came. They dragged us from our beds and forced us into a truck. My father tried to fight them. The soldiers beat him with their rifles.

"The truck was full of people moaning and wailing. They shoved us inside and slammed the tailgate. My father was unconscious. My mother and grandmother tried to stop the blood gushing from his head. I hugged my brothers and sisters, struggling to keep my balance as the truck pulled away.

"Over and over again the truck stopped. More and more people were shoved inside until we were packed so tightly that we couldn't raise our arms. Late the next day they finally let us out.

"'Don't be afraid,' the soldiers said. 'You're going on a train to Thailand, where you'll be safe.' They led us across a field to the edge of the woods. There were no train tracks; there was no train—only shovels. They told us to dig a trench. We asked why. 'Keep digging,' they said. There weren't enough shovels, so we used our hands. Even my grandmother and baby sister had to dig.

"Then they started shooting. Bullets sprayed everywhere. One of the first bullets found my mother. It hit her so hard that she was knocked backward. She fell on top of me, pinning me down. I couldn't move. The loose dirt from the trench filled my mouth. The guns sounded like firecrackers. One after another, people fell into the pit, screaming, calling out to each other. And then the guns stopped. I tried to wiggle out from under my mother. 'Make sure they're all dead,' I heard the leader say. 'Fill in the hole when you're done.'

"My mother's blood was hot on my back. It was dripping down my neck into my ears. I didn't dare move.

"The soldiers worked their way through the trench, turning over bodies, clubbing people, silencing the cries with their guns. Somehow they missed me. They shoveled the dirt back into the trench. I heard their laughter as they marched away. I was afraid to move. I lay there until I couldn't stand it anymore. Then I dug my way out. I climbed into a tree to hide. Below me, in a long grave thinly blanketed with dirt, were my mother, father, three sisters, two brothers, aunt, and grandmother—all dead."

The boy fell to his knees, his arms hanging limp at his sides. He looked up at me. The glazed look was gone. I was looking into the eyes of my old playmate from Small Bor.

"Khoy," I whispered. "It's me, Mok." I wrapped him in my arms.

Chapter Thirty-Two
Leaving Battambang

Rations were cut and then cut again as we entered the rainy season. Khoy and I foraged outside the *wat* as often as we were allowed, but because the soldiers could get water by catching the rain, they didn't let us come and go as freely as they had before.

Tormented by hunger, we'd spy on the Khmer Rouge families, waiting for a chance to steal their food. We watched a mother give her children three dead chickens. "Take these away and bury them," she said.

"Those chickens must be diseased, or they would've eaten them," I said.

"I don't care," said Khoy. "They might not be good enough for Khmer Rouge children, but they're fine for us."

After the children left, we dug up the chickens. We smuggled them into the *wat* hidden under our clothes.

People smelled them cooking. They shoved Khoy and me aside and ripped the fowl from the fire. We fought to keep the chickens, but there were too many people kicking, grabbing, and hitting us with sticks. When it was over, there wasn't so much as a wing for Khoy and me to share.

By daylight, people everywhere were vomiting, doubled over in pain from eating the chickens. Some of them became so ill that they were sent back to the hospital.

"There will be a meeting at sunset," the Pol Pots announced. "Everyone must attend."

Why were they calling a meeting now? We had never had a meeting at the *wat* before. Would we be taken away? Killed? A woman hid her baby in the trash pile. Another walked beside the fence, circling the *wat* over and over. Every so often she bent down, dug a shallow hole, and buried one of her treasures. A man sat in a corner, rocking back and forth, back and forth. We waited and wondered.

Rainwater dripped down on us through the holes in the temple roof. We sat motionless in rows while the soldiers made their inspection. One of them hoisted himself onto the stone base of a fallen Buddha. "*Angka* is not pleased," he shouted. "*Angka* needs rice to help make Kampuchea great again. You lie around doing nothing all day, eating well, while the true workers for *Angka* are starving. This must stop! If you want to eat, you must work. Return to your camps now!"

The one-eyed man leaned toward me. "We must leave," he whispered. "They'll kill whoever stays behind."

The one-eyed man had spent his entire life in the *wat*. Since he had no camp to return to, I asked him to come with us, but he just shook his head and wandered away.

The city was quiet as we were marched away except for a smattering of Khmer Rouge children clamoring among the ruins that had once been the bustling buildings of

Battambang. They didn't have swollen bellies. They ran and played while Khoy and I could barely lift one foot in front of the other.

We followed the highway to Phnom Pong. The Khmer Rouge moved people around so often that all I could hope was that Luon, Veun, and the girls were still there.

Every eight kilometers we came to a checkpoint where we had to show the papers that the soldiers had given us when we'd left the *wat*. At one post we were stopped by a guard no older than us.

"Where are you going?" he asked.

"We are going home from the hospital," I answered.

"Let me have your pass," demanded the boy.

We handed the boy our papers. He squinted at them. It was obvious that he couldn't read—he was holding the papers upside down!

"Wait here!" he ordered. He took our papers and left. We could feel black eyes watching us as we waited. After more than an hour, the boy returned. "Okay," he said, handing the papers back to us. "You can go."

As darkness descended, we reached the outskirts of the city.

"I can't see to go on," I said, once again plagued by night blindness. "Let's stop here."

While Khoy left to scrounge up something to eat, I crawled under a battered car and waited.

"Mok!" Khoy shouted. "Come quick!"

I jumped to my feet.

"Hurry!" he called. "Just ahead of you on the left."

I strained to see him in the dark, but everything was shadow. I stumbled onward, every few seconds calling his name and creeping forward as he answered.

Suddenly, I slipped. Splash! I fell headlong into tepid water. As I sputtered to the surface, I heard Khoy's laughter.

"It's an American swimming pool!" he called. Running to the edge of the bomb crater, Khoy jumped in beside me.

Chapter Thirty-Three
A Place to Sleep

The horrors of the past few years faded as Khoy and I left Battambang behind. Intoxicated with freedom, we joked and teased like we had in Small Bor.

Our euphoria soon faded. The grinding pains in our stomachs reminded us that we'd eaten our last meal, a half can of watery soup, the previous morning. While we walked, we searched for anything edible. The rice paddies were picked clean. The trees had been stripped of bark, their branches bare of even unripened fruit. Animals slow enough to be caught had long since been devoured. Aside from a few crickets and worms, we found nothing. Like us, everyone in Kampuchea had become vultures, scavenging to stay alive.

Sundown found us on a deserted dirt road in the hill country southwest of Battambang. The going was slow and difficult as we made our way through thorn bushes, weeds, and tree roots until the road disappeared completely. We stopped to rest and wait for the stars to guide us.

But that night there were no stars. When the night noises began, fear of wild animals and ghosts drove us to our feet. Half walking, half crawling, we groped our way up a rise.

Below, beckoning us, the valley was aglow with flickering cook fires. We hid behind some rocks and watched the camp. The smell of fish cooking filled my nostrils. Hunger overcame my fear.

"Maybe they'll give us something to eat," I suggested.

"Or maybe they'll kill us," said Khoy.

"Either way, it doesn't matter," I said. "We'll die if we don't get something to eat."

Head lowered, I put my hands together like the monks had taught me. I knew that the people might kill me, but I couldn't stop myself. I walked up to one of the houses. A Khmer Rouge family was eating, their plates piled with food. Humbly, I fell to my knees. One of the women took pity on me. She laid a bowl of rice and fish and kim chee outside the door. Khoy squatted beside me, and we ate.

When we were finished, the woman led us to a long bamboo building built above a fallow rice paddy. We climbed up the ladder and followed her inside. The front half of the building was piled high with bags of rice and canned foods. She lifted the edge of a green and yellow *krama* hanging from the ceiling. A dozen pairs of eyes met mine. She nudged aside a tiny boy and motioned for us to lie down. "You can sleep here," she said.

I couldn't force my eyes to close. Illuminated by candlelight, brightly colored labels glowed. I traced the Chinese characters on the cans of mandarin oranges, lychee nuts, and jackfruit, planning how we could smuggle some out when we left the next day.

Chapter Thirty-Four
The Good Life

Before we left the next morning, Khoy and I stopped to say goodbye to the woman who'd helped us. Her husband was there.

"Why are you leaving?" he asked. "Stay here in Po Kapber. We have plenty of work for you."

Though the man's words were quietly spoken, I knew they were a command. Besides, I wasn't sure we'd be able to find my family. My belly was full, and I had a safe place to sleep. Life here was already better than in the hospital, the *wat*, or the other camps.

Khoy joined the line of children waiting for breakfast while I took our *kramas* back to the warehouse. Stealthily, I replaced the canned goods I had taken.

"We walked here from the *wat* in Battambang," Khoy was explaining to another boy as he made room for me in line. "How did you get here?"

"Mir Tuck brought us in a truck."

The boy who said this was about my age. He was Hmong. I could tell because he spoke with the distinctive coarse accent of those mountain people.

"Mir, your uncle?" asked Khoy. "And the woman who fed us is your aunt?"

The children giggled.

"Oh, no. He's not really our uncle. We call him *Mir* because he is like an uncle. Our parents were Khmer Rouge fighters. When Lon Nol's soldiers killed them, Mir Tuck and his wife brought us here to live."

"This used to be a market," the tallest boy informed us. "Chinaman, the cook, owned it. After we won the war, Mir Tuck took it away from him. Now the market is our camp. It takes its name from Po Kapber." He pointed to the mountain we'd climbed the night before. "The giant crocodile protects our camp."

While we ate, Khoy joked with the orphans. He was his old self again—the friend I'd played with, the boy who'd hidden with me in the tops of trees at the marketplace, spitting seeds on the shoppers.

Flies competed with us for the food. A big, fat, green one landed on my dish. I smacked it. The dish flipped; my food flew. The boys convulsed with laughter as I scooped up the dirty noodles.

"Do you want to climb Po Kapber's back?" the tall boy asked.

"Sure," said Khoy, already one of the group. "Let's go." I wanted to go with them, but caution held me back.

When they returned, Khoy was jubilant. Sok, the tall boy and leader of the group, had taken a liking to him. That night, Khoy moved his mat next to Sok's.

After that, Khoy spent most of his time with Sok and the others. To keep myself from thinking about my mother or worrying about Luon and my cousins, I explored the valley.

A few kilometers from camp was a rice paddy. Lying on my belly in the grass, I watched the workers. Heads covered with woven grass hats, backs bowed, ragged pants rolled above their knees, they sloshed through the muddy water. One by one they pulled pale green shoots from their packs and pushed them into the soggy soil. A worker fell behind. The Khmer Rouge guards screamed and gleefully prodded the offender with their guns. Dodging the onslaught, the chastised worker plunged the shoots into the soil at an even faster pace. *That could be me,* I thought, *if it weren't for Mir Tuck and his wife.*

The work Mir Tuck gave us was easy. Our main job was tending the vegetable garden. Two Khmer Rouge boys, Tek and Phan, were assigned to keep an eye on us. A couple of times a day they strutted by, brandishing their guns and shoving us around. But we weren't scared of them; they just liked to play soldier.

.   .   .

Though there was plenty of food, I never seemed to get enough. Half an oil drum full of rice was always cooking over the fire in Chinaman's hut—so much rice, bubbling and gurgling in the pot. Whether I was on my way to weed the garden or carry water for Mir Tuck, I couldn't stop myself from passing by.

"Hey, *boun!*" Chinaman shouted, referring to my swollen stomach. "Bring me some firewood, and I'll give you a fish ball."

Long after plenty of good food flattened my stomach, Chinaman continued to call me "balloon belly."

Khoy didn't understand why I spent so much time with Chinaman. "Come with us to the bat caves," he urged.

I shook my head. "Chinaman's teaching me to make kim chee."

"He can teach you another time," said Khoy.

"Mok's head is too pickled to shoot straight," said Phan. Sok, Tek, and even Khoy laughed at Phan's joke.

"We'll have more fun without him," said Sok, pulling Khoy away. "I'll let you use my slingshot."

I watched them leave. Why couldn't Khoy see how Sok was trying to separate us?

•   •   •

I wasn't the only one who hung around the kitchen. Mir Tuck's pet monkey was always begging for a handout. While Chinaman and I worked, the monkey pushed his scrunched-up old man's face into mine and chattered. I answered his monkey talk, and he nodded his head like we were having a real conversation. Sitting on my shoulder, he picked through my hair with his tiny claws. Each time he found a louse or a flea, he squealed with delight. But he didn't clean my head for nothing. When he dug in my pocket, he expected to find a treat. Cucumbers were his favorite. If my pockets were empty, he shook his fists and scolded me, screeching louder when I laughed.

In the middle of the kitchen was a long wooden table where the soldiers ate. I ran away whenever the soldiers were around, afraid they'd give me trouble. Once, I stayed too long. A patrol came in. Before I could get away, they spotted me.

"Who's the boy?" one of them asked. He pushed me aside and dipped his bowl in the pot. I didn't know what to do. I pretended to be dumb. I slouched, grasped the stirring stick with both hands, and let my tongue fall from my mouth.

"He's one of Mir Tuck's orphans," explained Chinaman. The soldier held my head in his hands and examined my face. "He doesn't look Khmer to me."

I smiled and gurgled, ignoring his fingers digging into my scalp.

"He's an empty head," said Chinaman, "but for a little rice, he works hard."

"We work hard, too!" said the other soldiers. "Where's our rice?"

Chinaman hurried to fill their bowls.

"How many did we kill today?"

"Only three. The last one didn't die easy."

"Did you see the way Chorb danced, trying to miss being kicked by the woman's foot when I tied the bag around her head?"

The soldiers laughed.

A skinny, narrow-eyed soldier shoved the man next to him. "It wasn't her kick I was dodging," Chorb said. "It was the piss running down her leg. I didn't want to get my feet wet!"

I closed my ears to their killing stories. *You are alive,* I said to myself. *You have plenty to eat; you have a place to sleep; you don't slave in the rice paddies.* Soundlessly, invisibly, I stirred the rice.

Chapter Thirty-Five
The Bicycle Ride

I was gathering wood for Chinaman when I saw Gianh, Mir Tuck's son, sitting on the root of a banyan tree.

"*Met*," he called. "I've been scouring the area for traitors. I'm tired and hungry. Get me a mango."

"Chinaman needs this wood," I said, shifting the heavy load of sticks.

"I want a mango now!" he demanded.

There was a mango tree only a few feet from where Gianh was sitting. I set down my load and plucked a soft, orangey one. He examined it, then tossed it over his shoulder.

"I want one of those," he said, pointing to a cluster of ripe fruit at the top of the tree.

I didn't want to anger Gianh, or he might report me to his father. I climbed into the tree and picked the mangoes he wanted. On the way down, I startled a nesting bird. It flew in my face. I lost my grip and tumbled down, landing in a thorn bush. I held out my arm to Gianh. "Help me," I said.

Gianh just laughed, took the mangoes, and left.

The angry Chinaman, wondering where his wood was, freed me from the thorny prison.

When he had nothing better to do, Gianh pestered Chinaman.

"We want to help," he said, leaning his gun against the kitchen wall. His younger brother, Sem, was with him. Sem was about Saveun's age. But instead of being a shriveled bag of bones, he was chubby and giggly.

"Let us help," Sem pleaded, grabbing Chinaman around the waist.

"I'm busy." Chinaman swatted him away like a pesky fly.

Gianh started stripping the husk from an ear of corn. "Give me that!" said Chinaman. "You'll only make a mess."

Chinaman tried to take the corn away. Gianh and Sem ran around him, ducking and dodging. He chased them. I could tell that this was a game they'd played many times. I stirred the rice, pretending not to watch.

Chinaman threw up his hands. "If I open a can of fruit, will you leave me alone?" he asked.

They bobbed their heads in agreement.

Chinaman led the way to the warehouse. He scanned the piles of cans, stroking his chin. He selected one. We held our breath as he turned it over in his hand. With a shake of his head, he replaced it.

"Pick the pineapple! Pick the pineapple!" Sem squealed. Chinaman glanced at him, then turned his attention back to the cans. Gianh knew better than to call out a favorite. If he did, Chinaman would take even longer to choose.

It seemed like forever before Chinaman made his choice. "*Angka* won't miss this small can of pineapple," he said.

Like the other Khmer Rouge children, Gianh carried an AK-47 and acted like a soldier. There was never a button missing on his clean, black uniform. Once, when he stepped in a pile of animal dung, he flung his sandals into a wild potato patch.

"I don't want these smelly sandals anymore!" he said.

I looked at my scarred, mud-caked feet. "May I have them, comrade?"

"Take them," he said. "My father will give me a new pair."

Because his father was the camp leader, Gianh could do whatever he wanted. His only job was to keep the camp ducks out of the rice paddies and make sure eagles or snakes didn't steal their ducklings. He made me take his place whenever Mir Tuck was away. He and Sem had great fun riding their bicycles through the group of ducks when I was on guard.

"Quack, quack, quack!" the brothers screamed, weaving wildly around me.

Squawking and flapping, the frightened birds scattered, trying to escape the oncoming wheels. One of the ducks got away. Laughter followed me as I chased it into a thicket. I knew I'd be punished if the duck was lost. Ignoring the razor-sharp leaves slashing my flesh, I searched for the bird.

Finally, I gave up. It was too dark. My legs and arms throbbing, flies biting at my wounds, terrified of what Mir

Tuck would do to me, I returned to camp. Gianh was waiting for me.

"I've been looking everywhere for you," he said. "Where's the duck?"

"I couldn't find it," I said. "What will your father do when he finds out?"

"I'll tell him wolves ate it," said Gianh.

The next time I saw Gianh, I was carrying water to the garden. He and six other Khmer Rouge kids were riding their bicycles. They circled me, making the ring smaller and smaller until I had to stop.

Gianh jumped off his bicycle and pushed it toward me. "Ride my bike," he said.

I just looked at him. I didn't know how to ride, and he knew it. He had offered to let me ride his bicycle many times while I was watching the ducks.

"Ride my bike!" he ordered. Then, in a threatening whisper, he said, "If you don't, I'll tell my father you ate the duck!"

I climbed onto the bicycle. As soon as I put my feet on the pedals, it tipped over. The kids were hysterical.

"Do it again!" Gianh demanded.

Over and over, Gianh made me get back on the bicycle. Each time the kids laughed when I fell off. Finally, they tired of the game and left me alone.

Chapter Thirty-Six
Ant Wars

"The black ant is mine," said Sok, drawing a small circle in the moist, black dirt beneath the warehouse. "The red ant's yours."

Languorous from the heat, I stared at the rotting floorboards overhead.

Phan nudged me. "Hurry up!" he said. "Put yours in the middle."

Khoy and the Hmong boy banged bamboo sticks against the stilts supporting the warehouse. "Start the war!" they shouted.

I placed the red ant in the circle, and Sok put his black one on its back.

"Red ants are Lon Nol's army. They are big and clumsy," said Sok. "Black ants are Khmer. They're stronger and faster. Watch!"

The boys cheered as the insects battled. Finally, the black ant bit the long legs off the red ant.

"I told you!" yelled Sok. "The Khmer always win!"

"Go find more red ants," Tek commanded me.

When I came back, two more ants were at war. I set the can of red ants beside Tek and walked away.

Khoy followed me. "Why are you leaving?"

"I don't want to play ant wars," I said. "The black ant always wins, and Sok always has to have the black ant."

"You never want to do anything," said Khoy. "You act stupid all the time and let everyone make fun of you. You carry pebbles for Sok's slingshot. You think if you give him rocks, he'll be nice to you, but he just laughs at you. They like me. I don't let them use me. They're my friends."

"They may laugh at me, but I have enough to eat and a place to sleep," I said. "You think they're your friends, but you can't trust them. They're Khmer Rouge, and we're not. Any moment they could kill you."

"You're just jealous!" shouted Khoy. "Your only friends are an old Chinaman and a monkey!"

That night I was nervous about going to dinner. I wasn't sure how Khoy would act after our fight.

"It's so hot, everyone's eating under the warehouse," said Khoy, acting as though we hadn't quarreled. Knowing that I couldn't see in the dark, he walked beside me like he usually did. He held my bowl and helped me find a place to sit. The kids were talking about a wild pig hunt that the soldiers were planning.

"We carry the guns," said Phan. "Maybe they'll let you carry one, too, Mok."

I was surprised at how friendly Phan was being. "I hope so," I said.

"Try the rice," said the Hmong boy. "It has pieces of boar meat in it."

I scooped a big spoonful from my bowl and put it in my mouth. "Aaarrgghhh!" I sputtered. My bowl of rice had been switched for one full of dirt.

The boys laughed uproariously as I spewed mud out of my mouth. Khoy laughed the loudest. He hadn't forgotten our fight. He'd told the others that I couldn't see in the dark.

Chapter Thirty-Seven
Climbing Trees

I lay on my back, shaded by the dark green leaves of the mango tree. If I were still living in the children's camp at Srai Bun Jul, the golden mangoes, just beginning to redden, wouldn't be hanging from the trees; neither would the green banana stalks, nor the leathery-husked coconuts. Before they were a quarter of the size they are now, we would have picked and eaten them—anything to fill our bellies, even if stomach cramps were the price we'd pay.

I swung onto a branch. Mir Ton had taught me to climb trees almost before I could walk. Standing in his uniform below a milkfruit tree, he had coached me while I clung to the trunk.

"Don't hug it with your feet like you do to climb a papaya tree," he said. "Grab the branches, and see how quickly you will climb."

I was a fast learner.

"Only climb trees you can trust," he told me. "Ones that will hold you up."

Mir Ton had let me sleep in the treetops. The wind blew, and the branches swayed, rocking me to sleep.

After the Khmer Rouge took over, I stopped climbing trees for fun. We needed the fruit to stay alive.

The rhythmic squeak of Gianh's bicycle brought me back to Po Kapber Camp. I picked the best mangoes and jumped down. "Come with me," he ordered. "We need water."

Sitting in front of one of the huts along the river was an old woman chewing betel nuts. Her lips and chin were stained brown from the juice.

"Hey," she called out. "Are you another one of Mir Tuck's orphans?"

Gianh hid behind me and answered, "Yes."

"Come closer," said the old woman. "I want to get a better look at you."

Gianh pushed me ahead of him. If anyone was going to be in trouble, he wanted it to be me.

"Are you a good boy?" she asked. A black stream of juice dripped onto her lap.

"Yes, grandmother," I answered respectfully.

"You be good," she admonished, "because Mir Tuck is good to you, and you're lucky he took you in."

"Mok's good. Mok's good and stupid," Gianh taunted once we were out of hearing range. "The last time I passed her hut, she threw a coconut at me."

•　　•　　•

I watched as a rivalry developed between Khoy and Sok. Everything they did became a contest: Who could run the fastest? Who caught the most fish? Who planted the most seeds? Who carried the most water? When the camp needed new latrines, they even competed to see who could dig the deepest hole.

One night their rivalry stopped being a game.

"I can climb a tree faster than you!" shouted Khoy.

"No, you can't!" countered Sok.

"Yes, I can!" Khoy retorted.

Sok jumped on Khoy, and the two fell to the ground, wrestling. A crowd formed, cheering as the boys kicked and gouged each other.

Finally, Mir Tuck broke through the circle and pulled them apart. "I know how to settle this," he said. "We'll have a competition."

Khoy and Sok were about the same size, both of them taller than I was, and strong. Sok looked mightier. It was obvious that he had never had to eat ants to stay alive.

So they decided to have a race to the top of a tree the next day. Khoy begged me to teach him to climb faster. I kept telling him, "It's better to lose. This isn't just a game to Sok." But he wouldn't leave me alone until I agreed.

Everyone in the camp came to watch. Mir Tuck had chosen the two tallest palms in the grove for the contest. He and the other soldiers made bets. It was clear from the wagers that Sok was the favorite.

Mir Tuck fired his pistol. Khoy and Sok each ran to a tree. About halfway up, Khoy started to pull ahead. The frenzied crowd urged Sok to climb faster. He slipped. He hugged the tree with his knees and regained his balance.

Silently, I screamed for Khoy to lose. But he didn't.

After that, things changed for Khoy. The orphans peed on his grass mat and spit in his food bowl. Mir Tuck singled him out for any nasty job. And Sok started paying attention to me.

Chapter Thirty-Eight
The Bat Cave

"Have you ever eaten a bat?" Sok asked. "I know where we can find some."

My pockets, heavy with pebbles, beat against my thighs as I followed Sok up the winding path. When we were almost to the top of a cliff, we climbed onto a ledge.

The stale, moist air of the cave hit me. At first all I could see as we stumbled into the blackness was the flickering yellow light of the candles that Sok and I carried. Gradually my eyes adjusted, and I began to make out the craggy, wet contours of the cavern. It was the first time I'd ventured into a dark place since the night they'd switched my bowl. I was surprised at how much my vision had improved since I'd started eating better.

"The bats sleep hanging from the top," said Sok, stretching the band on his slingshot. "I'll flush them out from the back."

Shielding the flame, I moved the candle from side to side in front of me. Close to the walls, the floor was littered with bones. In some places they had been heaped together in piles. Skulls, packed into cracks in the cave wall, stared back at me, jaws hanging open. I pulled the light away. It fell on a mound of orange, brown-stained rags. I knew then that the skulls and bones were the remains of monks.

I leaned against the wall of the cave to steady myself. Water ran from it onto my arm and dripped off my elbow. The heavy moisture pressed in on me. I could hear my breath echoing in my ears. I shivered.

"Are you cold?" asked Sok, startling me.

"Yes," I answered, not wanting him to know I was scared.

"The back of the cave is full of bats," he said. "Bring the rocks, and come on."

I backed away from the wall. Though I stepped carefully, I could feel the bones crunching beneath my feet.

Chapter Thirty-Nine
Hunting on Phnom Koy

Chinaman wrapped the last of the rice balls in banana leaves. I ran to the center of camp and gave them to the women stuffing *kramas* with supplies. Grabbing a bladder full of water, I joined the rest of the kids buzzing around the soldiers. I didn't want to miss the wild pig hunt.

When the soldiers finished checking their rifles and ammunition, they filed out. Half skipping, half running, we fell in behind them.

"Where do you think you're going?" asked Mir Tuck's wife, jerking a bladder from Khoy's hand. "Birds are attacking the rice, and you think you can go pig hunting? Stay here and guard the field!"

Climbing the curved, ridged trail up Po Kapber, I looked down at Khoy, a tiny scarecrow waving his arms in the middle of the rice paddy.

Sok caught up to one of the soldiers. "Can I carry your M16?" he asked.

The soldier thrust the heavy gun at Sok. Stumbling back, Sok settled it on his shoulder.

"I want to carry a gun, too," said Tek.

"Me, too," chorused the others.

We crowded around the soldiers. Finally, all of the boys had guns except me.

"You want to carry a gun, *met*?" asked Comrade Chorb.

"Yes," I answered, eagerly holding out my arms.

Chorb sniggered. "I'd never let you carry my gun, dumb boy! You're so clumsy, you'd drop it and shoot someone!" He pushed me aside.

Everyone laughed. I laughed, too, pretending not to know that they were making fun of me.

The farther we got from camp and Mir Tuck, the sillier everyone became. The soldiers reminded me of boys my sisters had flirted with at parties in Vietnam. They laughed, joked, and made up songs to sing while we walked.

When we reached the top of Po Kapber, the hunting party stopped to rest. The valley stretched for miles below us.

"There's Phnom Koy," announced Gianh, pointing to a bump in the valley floor. "Look how it sticks up out of the ground with nothing around it."

"That's why it's called Knot Mountain," said Phan.

"Let's go," said Gianh. "The sooner we get there, the sooner we can start hunting!"

Phnom Koy was covered with jungle. Using long, sharp *parangs*, the soldiers hacked a path through the undergrowth. We struggled to keep up. Vines as thick as Chinaman's thigh, curling around trees and over rocks, tried to trip us. Tall, spindly fromager trees jutted through the canopy of overhanging branches. I couldn't see gibbons, but I could hear them chattering; leaves rustled as they followed our passage from above. Vermillion, orange, and gold-speckled butterflies as large as parrots floated past us.

Comrade Bopha twirled slowly, her head thrown back, her face aglow in the hazy green light. "I haven't seen a forest this lush since before the bombs fell," she said.

I too was mesmerized by the beauty of the forest. Picking a purple flower, I crushed the cool petals to my face. Its scent reminded me of a tiny bottle of perfume my mother had.

"Look at this fig!" Comrade Bopha hugged a thick, gray-white tree; its branches spread above us like a parasol. Picking the plump green orb, she sank her teeth into the soft fruit. The juice ran down her chin.

Following her lead, we stuffed ourselves with figs, berries, mushrooms, nuts, and wild onions.

"Slow down," she said, laughing. "You're going to get sick from eating so much."

We couldn't stop. We crammed our mouths and filled our shirts for later.

We set up camp near a stream. We laid our sleeping mats on a bed of moss where the water trickled through the cracks in a fern-covered rock.

"Hurry up," said Chorb, "or it'll be too dark to hunt."

"Too much fruit," grumbled Comrade Bopha. Our bloated bellies told us she was right.

"Pretty soon they'll be heading for the bushes," she added.

Sweat broke out on my forehead. I doubled over in pain.

Gianh was the first to go. I went next. Squatting in the bush, we could hear the soldiers heckling us, warning of porcupines, wolves, and snakes that would squeeze our guts.

Comrade Kru took pity on us. "My father and grandfather were Kru Khmer," he explained, crushing a caterpillar. "Though I was only a child when I became a soldier, I remember what they taught me." He smeared the caterpillar pulp on our bellies.

We were left behind when the soldiers went bird hunting, too sick to leave camp. Every few minutes, one of us roused himself to crawl into the bushes. In an effort to shut out the sounds of our bodies rebelling, I concentrated on the sounds of the forest.

"*Tekah, tekah.*" Hearing the lizard call, I remembered a game I had played with Pheap and Saveun. At night, in bed, we listened to the lizards talk to each other and mimicked them. "I'll marry; I'll not marry; I'll marry; I'll not marry." I fell asleep playing the game.

·   ·   ·

The wild pig, long snout pointed skyward, charged the tree. Froth hung from his blood-flecked whiskers. His pained, high-pitched cries echoed through the clearing. Tossing his head, the boar gouged the earth with his hooves and drove his tusks into the rubber tree. Tek and Gianh, who had taken refuge in the tree when they saw the wounded pig, struggled to maintain their grip. The tree thrashed wildly each time the boar hammered its trunk.

A soldier crept up behind the boar and cocked her rifle. From behind a thicket, we watched her shove the gun against the boar's sharp, spiny back. Sok clutched my arm as the soldier slowly squeezed the trigger.

We tied bamboo poles together with vine and hoisted the pig onto it. It took all of us to drag the pig, but we were happy to do it, our mouths already watering with the thought of the coming feast.

"When we get back to camp, I'm going to throw myself in the stream and lay there until my fingers are so shriveled they look like Chinaman's skin," panted Comrade Kru, lifting the *travois* over a clump of roots.

"You'd better get there before I do," said Chorb, "because I'm going to drink it all!"

We followed the stream to the base of a cliff. From hundreds of feet overhead, water plunged into a pool so clear that we could see suckerfish clinging to the bottom. Dropping their guns, Comrade Chorb and Comrade Kru dove into the emerald pool. We dove in after them.

The soldiers were sated long before we were. They watched us frolic in the cool spray, laughing when we ducked behind the waterfall to take our pants down and cool our sore, red bottoms on the rocks.

The female soldiers lay side by side on the bank. Their uniforms, still wet, were molded to their bodies. I couldn't help noticing the way the cloth hugged their skin. I turned over and buried my face in my arms. I knew that if anyone saw me looking at the women, I'd be punished.

Chapter Forty
Ghost Stories

Chorb hacked hunks of meat from the hog's haunches and skewered them on a branch, which he laid across the fire. We took turns turning the spit. Flames jumped up, licking the juices that dripped from the roasting meat. Gianh fanned the fire with a banana leaf so it would burn hotter and we could eat sooner.

Night fell quickly. Licking the last of the hog juices from our fingers, we lay back on our mats. The heavy air wrapped around us like a blanket. The soldiers, outlined against the purple night, sat around the fire.

"Why did you bury the hog's hooves, Kru?" asked Chorb. "Chinaman could use them to flavor rice and soup."

Kru poked the fire with a stick. "If you don't bury some part of the animal, its spirit can't rest."

The Hmong boy agreed. "The spirit will follow you on the hunt and scare away the animals."

"Once, when I was small, my grandfather was called to the home of a man whose daughters had been taken over by evil spirits," said Kru. "The girls were writhing on the floor, holding their heads. When my grandfather entered the hut, the girls jumped up. Their mouths were twisted. They were babbling. One of them had a deep voice like a man's. The other had a high, shrill voice that made my flesh crawl.

"'Where do you come from?' my grandfather asked. 'How did you get here?'

"'We come by lake,' the girls answered.

"'Why are you here?' my grandfather continued.

"The girl with the deep voice answered, 'We are looking for cats and dogs and chicken blood to feed our two children waiting for us by the rice paddy.' They tried to leave.

"'Don't go!' ordered my grandfather. 'Why have you taken over these girls' bodies?'

"'We've been murdered,' said the high-voiced girl. 'We want revenge.'

"My grandfather tied the girls' hands behind their backs and secured them to a pole. 'You can go, but you can't take these bodies with you,' he said.

"The girls screamed. Their heads fell to their chests, and their eyes closed. I was so scared that I cried for my grandfather to leave. He sat on the floor in a trance. About an hour later, the girls woke up. They didn't remember anything, and their headaches were gone."

"How did the ghosts get into the girls' bodies?" asked Tek.

"They entered their bodies between their toes," answered Kru.

I wrapped my feet with my *krama* and held them tightly. I could hear the other boys rustling around. They were covering their feet, too.

A soldier leaned forward, her face glowing orange for a moment as she pulled a stick from the fire and lit her *kai* leaf cigarette. "Once, when we were hiding in the hills," she said, exhaling, "two of us were sent to guard a bridge overnight. I took the first watch while my partner slept. When it was time for her to take over, I shook her. She sat up, holding her arms out like a zombie.

"'It's your turn to watch the bridge,' I said.

"'This is my home,' she answered in a slow monotone. She looked at me. I could tell she didn't know who I was. I was frightened, and I ran back to my group. We sent for a Kru Khmer.

"'Why did you come into this girl?' he asked my partner.

"'I needed a place to rest,' answered the ghost.

"'You cannot stay in this girl,' said the Kru. 'Leave her!'

"The ghost refused. The Kru wrapped a plastic bag around the girl's neck and started choking the ghost out of her. Gasping and kicking, the girl struggled to free herself until her eyes rolled back in her head, and all I could see was the white part.

"'Stop!' shouted the ghost. 'I'll leave!'

"When the Kru removed the plastic bag, the girl woke up. She remembered nothing."

Chorb stood up and peered into the jungle. "Look at that tree!" he whispered. "There's a ghost lady trapped in it!"

The soldiers crept closer for a better look.

"I see her! She has long teeth like a horse."

"Her hair hangs down to her knees."

"She's feeding a baby!"

Too frightened to look, the rest of us scooted closer to the fire. The cries of owls and cicadas, so pleasant earlier, became menacing. I plugged my ears and closed my eyes. It was a long time before I fell asleep.

Brave once daylight came, we dared to approach the tree. We examined it from every angle, but the lady and her baby were gone. All that was left was a gnarled tree trunk.

Chapter Forty-One
The Deer Hunt

On the last day of the hunt, we came upon a doe with her wobbly-legged fawn, drinking from a spring. The mother's ears pricked up, and she turned our way, her nose twitching, ready to run. We held our breath. Thinking she was safe, the doe went back to drinking.

The Hmong boy tiptoed toward the pair, hoping to touch a soft, velvety back. Just beyond his fingertips, the doe started and bolted into the brush, followed by her baby.

Chorb pushed the Hmong boy to the ground. "If you hadn't scared them away, that doe would've been mine!" he yelled.

We were sent into the woods, like hunting dogs, to flush out the deer. Mice scampered away from our flying feet. Wild chickens and families of pheasants flew from our path. Then we spotted a herd of deer. Leaping over vines and ducking under branches, we chased the deer. For a moment I was one of them, bounding toward death.

When the soldiers started shooting, I dove under a bush. Bullets sprayed everywhere, ricocheting off rocks, shattering tree limbs.

Chorb screamed. "My gun misfired!" he cried. His face was charred, the hair above his ear frizzled and burned white. Kru pried Chorb's bloody fingers loose from the gun. I could see pieces of bone and muscle where the flesh had been torn away.

Everyone was so busy worrying over Chorb that they didn't notice that Phan was missing. Tek found him. A bullet had blown off the side of his face.

"Take his shirt off," Bopha said, nudging Phan's body with her foot. "We need bandages."

Tek gulped hard.

"Why are you crying?" she asked. "If he'd watched where he was running, the deer would be dead instead of him." She jabbed Tek in the stomach with her gun. "You're so sorry for Phan, maybe you want to join him."

"No, no," said Tek, fumbling with the buttons on Phan's shirt. "I'm not crying, comrade. There's bark in my eye."

"Chorb's losing a lot of blood," said Kru. "Hurry up with those bandages."

We left Phan lying in the clearing where he'd fallen. We weren't allowed to cover him with rocks so the animals couldn't eat his body. Silently, I asked Buddha to watch over Phan's spirit.

On the way back to Po Kapber Camp, I carried Chorb's gun. The blue-gray steel was cold to the touch. I cradled the butt, rubbed smooth by Chorb's hand. *Dumb boy,* I could hear him saying. *You can't carry my gun. You'd drop it and shoot someone!*

I wanted to use the gun I was carrying. *I can shoot the soldiers and run away,* I thought. *Do I have enough bullets to shoot them all? What if I miss? What would they do to my family when they found out what I had done?*

When we got back to camp, I gave the gun to Chorb's wife.

Chapter Forty-Two
The Hungry Boy

"Chorb's arm will take a long time to heal," said Chorb's wife. "It is too much for me to care for him and two children. I've seen you orphan boys. All you do is play. You will stay here and help me until Chorb is well."

Chorb was no different at home than he'd been on the hunt. He kept me and his wife, Mien Chorb, running constantly—"Bring me this! Bring me that!" It seemed that no matter what I did, it was wrong. "Dumb boy, the soup is too hot!" he'd say, spitting it in my face. "Dumb boy, the cigarette is rolled too loosely. It won't stay lit!"

When Chorb's arm started to heal, it itched and almost drove him crazy. His sons, Khour and Wern, drove him crazy, too. It became my job to keep them out of his way. I clowned around with them. They liked me and laughed. Wern rode on my back and tugged on my ears.

When I had a few minutes to myself, I searched out Khoy. Mir Tuck had him digging a latrine. I made sure that no one was looking before I dared approach him. Watching him tip his scrawny neck to drink the water I brought and seeing the way he ripped apart the fruit I shared, I didn't need to ask how he was being treated.

After Chorb began to improve, I was sent back to the warehouse at night to sleep. Khoy would be waiting for me. Like a vulture, he'd devour the leftovers I brought from Chorb's house, but they weren't enough. He started sneaking out, taking milkfruit, mangoes, and bananas from the trees. I warned him not to go.

"What do you know?" he sneered. "Your belly is always full. The little bit of food you bring me isn't enough. I'll be back before you know it with lots to eat, and finally the pain in my stomach will be gone."

I rocked myself to sleep that night, waiting for Khoy to return.

I awoke when Mir Tuck and the soldiers stormed into the warehouse. "Get up and come with us!" they demanded, yanking all of us from sleep.

They marched us away from Po Kapber. With each step, I grew more and more scared. In other camps, when people were taken away, they didn't return. I fell to the back of the line. I didn't want to be one of the people who never came back. The others must have felt the same because they all slowed down.

We came to a halt at the edge of a harvested paddy. In the sea of dried, brownish spikes was a bamboo cage. Cowering inside was Khoy. His swollen face was bruised and bloody. One leg was twisted behind him.

The sharp rice chaff jabbed into my feet. I shifted my weight. I could see the spikes jutting through the floor of the cage. I knew they were jabbing into Khoy as well.

"Move closer," said Mir Tuck. "Get a good look at this boy. He's a thief. At night he's been sneaking into the jungle, stealing fruit. The fruit belongs to *Angka*. He has stolen from every one of us. He must be punished."

The soldiers passed out coconut shells and bamboo pipes. Mir Tuck opened the cage and dragged Khoy out. "Hit him!" he commanded.

Eagerly, Sok struck the first blow. The others joined in, laughing, while they beat Khoy.

Mir Tuck's black eyes bore into me. "He stole from you!" he shouted angrily. "Why aren't you hitting him? Are you a thief, too?"

My hand trembling, I swatted Khoy.

"Is that as hard as you can hit?"

I hit him again.

While Mir Tuck looked on, we flogged Khoy until he lay motionless on the ground.

For a week, I secretly nursed Khoy, washing his wounds and spooning water through his swollen, cracked lips. I woke in the night each time his moaning stopped, terrified that he was dead.

One night I woke to find him stuffing rice and cans in a basket.

"What are you doing?" I asked.

"I can't stay here anymore," he answered.

"How can you leave? You're too weak. Your leg isn't healed," I protested.

"I'll make it," he said. "Come with me. We'll find your family."

"Here I have all the food I can eat, and I don't have to work hard," I said.

"They tease you. They treat you worse than they do Mir Tuck's monkey," Khoy replied. "My family is dead. You're the only one I have left. Please come."

I didn't want to be separated from Khoy, and I longed to see Luon and the girls. But if I left Po Kapber, I knew that it would be just like it had been before: starving and slaving in the fields day and night. My throat was so tight that I couldn't speak. I shook my head and turned away.

"If I see Luon, I'll tell her you're living here so she won't worry," Khoy whispered in the darkness.

Chapter Forty-Three
Mir Tuck's Son

When the rain came, it was like none before. No days of heavy black skies warned us; no thunder rumbled in the distance; no scattered showers, lasting just long enough for us to wash ourselves and set pots under the roof, teased us. One day the sun rose blood-red and hot just like every day before. Then, about mid-afternoon, as though a *krama* had been pulled over and wrapped around the sun, the sky went black, and it rained. It gushed down the baked hillside, rushing onto the road, churning up the dirt in the rice paddies. Like someone had jabbed a hole in an oil drum, the rain poured down for weeks on end without a break, searching out every crack in our hut so that our sleeping mats, clothes, and even the ladder onto the hut sagged soggily.

I rolled up my pant legs and waded out in search of firewood. The path was a bubbling, oozing river of black mud. The branches I found crumbled under my touch. I searched deep in the forest for dry wood where the animals, birds, and bugs had hidden to wait out the torrent.

With the return of the rain came my malaria. I couldn't stop the fits of shaking and thrashing and dizziness. It was the worst bout I'd had. I flopped around like a fish. One day soldiers threw me into the back of a jeep. I thought they were going to take me to the fields and kill me. I fainted.

I woke up in a hospital. It was nothing like the hospital in Battambang. It was clean and quiet. A woman brought me some food and water. She lifted my head and held the cup to my lips.

"Drink this," she said. "Your father will be pleased to know that you are awake."

My father? I wondered.

"You were very sick," she continued. "Your father's jeep brought you here a few days ago. We gave you a shot to treat the malaria. Eat now. You'll be better soon."

They thought I was Mir Tuck's son!

I learned that I was in Siem Reap and that the hospital had been a school. Only Khmer Rouge officers and their families were treated there. I feigned sleep and listened to the conversations around me.

"Did you see the convoy of jeeps that arrived this morning?"

"Comrade Uy said it brought important officers to inspect the hospital."

"Maybe one of them is Pol Pot!"

"It's somebody important. Comrade Uy is making sure that the hospital is in perfect order."

My heart thumped hard against my chest. They would find out that I wasn't Mir Tuck's son. I had to leave before the inspection.

When the nurse stopped at my mat to give me medicine, I let her shake me a long time before I stirred. I didn't want her to think I'd overheard their conversation.

After the nurses were gone and the other patients in my room had fallen asleep, I jumped out the window and hid in some bushes. I waited until I saw the old man who carried the corpses riding by on his three-wheeled cycle. Dragging my leg, my back hunched over, I limped in front of his *cyclo-pousse*.

"They told me to go back to my camp," I lisped, with my tongue thick so I sounded stupid. "But I don't know which way to go."

"What's the name of your camp, *met*?" he asked.

"Phnom Pong," I answered, thinking it was my chance to return to Luon.

"I'll give you a ride to the highway," he said.

The stench of rotting flesh was so strong that I could barely breathe. *The old man's nose must not work,* I thought, climbing into his blood-smeared rickshaw.

Chapter Forty-Four
Family Reunion

I wished I'd stolen some food before I left the hospital because on the way to Phnom Pong there was nothing to eat. The road was lined with stumps; American bombs had long ago destroyed the trees. The animals were gone. There was only the falling rain and my feet sloshing in the mud.

It took many days to reach Phnom Pong. Luon was as overjoyed to see me as I was to see her. Everything around the camp was different. A canal, churning with water, had been dug through the center of it. A maze of crumbling dikes divided the land into patchwork squares.

Saveun was different, too. She was taller. Her hair, still chopped short, was shiny. Her eyes, pale gold like Luon's, smiled up at me. I winced when I saw an angry red burn on her neck. I reached toward the hard ridges on her neck. She pulled away from me.

"Boiling oil splashed on me," she explained, fingering the scars. "I work in the kitchen now. Ma works there, too."

Luon fixed me a bowl of rice, greens, and bamboo shoots cooked with pork and squash—just like the breakfasts she used to fix on the farm.

"Everything is better now. When I came back after Sinoeun was born," she said, holding her new daughter to her breast, "they put me to work caring for the babies and working in the kitchen, so we have food all the time. No more watery gruel. Pheap works, too. She carries wood. Sometimes she even catches a fish or two."

I couldn't imagine tiny Pheap big enough to carry wood.

"Veun was sent away with the other men to repair the dikes," Luon continued. "In the meetings, Comrade Muy tells us that the dikes are needed so we will have water to grow more rice for *Angka*. I don't know why they bother. The dikes collapse from the rains as fast as they fix them."

Sinoeun gurgled. Luon poked her finger into one of the dimples on the chubby-cheeked baby. "Though they're working the men from before light till after dark, Veun still makes the long trek back whenever they let him so he can see Sinoeun. She's a sweet baby and brings him much pleasure. When he's with her, he is the old Veun, singing and smiling. I think Sinoeun is the only thing keeping him going."

That night we huddled against the only dry wall in the hut. I told them about Chinaman and Mir Tuck's monkey. Leaving out the times when the boys were cruel and teased me, I told every funny story I could think of, not wanting to stop. It was so good to hear them laugh.

"Tell us again about the time Sem fell into the rice paddy," urged Pheap.

"When Sem stood up," I told her, "he was covered with mud—even his eyes and mouth and hair. 'Ghost! Ghost!' we screamed and ran away. He chased after us waving his arms and moaning."

"Ghost! Ghost!" the girls squealed.

Holding my arms out like a zombie, I chased them around the hut, moaning, until Luon stopped us. "Comrade Muy will expect his rice at dawn," said Luon, "and the fire has to be stoked."

Grudgingly, the girls unrolled their mats. Long after they were asleep, I stayed awake listening to their breathing, afraid that if I let myself sleep, I'd wake up and find that the night had been just another dream.

While everyone was at work, I decided to repair the roof. On the way to gather fronds, I saw Comrade Muy lying in a hammock strung between two palm trees. His belly was so large that it stretched the fabric of his shirt taut, leaving gaping holes between the buttons where the fat bubbled through. I made a wide circle around him. I was afraid that if I came too close, he'd recognize me.

Most of the huts were deserted. The few people I saw were either very old or very young. Soldiers had taken away the men and almost all of the children.

"Saveun was left behind because of her accident," Luon explained that evening. "When the Pol Pots saw the blackened, pus-filled craters on her neck and chest, they said she would die, and they left her."

"If they had sent me away," said Saveun, "I'd probably be dead like the children at Srai Bun Jul."

"What do you mean?" I asked.

"Srai Bun Jul is gone," she explained. "Comrade Muy told us that a disease killed the children."

I knew that the disease was the Khmer Rouge.

That night I dreamed I was back in Srai Bun Jul. I was at a meeting. Phally accused me of being with one of the girls. "I don't know her!" I cried. Crooked didn't believe me. He dragged me through the camp, along the bamboo sleeping platform, down the steps, out into the field. My mouth and eyes filled with water and dirt. He screamed at me, "*Angka* will forgive you if you confess." I could only shake my head. Soldiers tied me to a tree. Crooked, now snarling, his nostrils flaring, came toward me waving a bloody *parang*. I turned my head and saw the girl I had been accused of being with. It was Saveun! Her face was sliced open from the corner of her mouth across her neck. I screamed.

Luon shook me awake. "You're having a bad dream," she said. "I'm not sleeping well either. Come outside with me."

Her presence calmed me. We sat for a long time, enjoying the closeness.

"Is Po Kapber a nice place?" she asked.

"Yes," I said. "I have plenty to eat."

"Do you have to work hard?"

"I work in a soldier's house. I help his wife and look after his children. It is easy."

"Then you must go back," said Luon. "If Comrade Muy finds you here, he will send you to another camp because you are too old to stay with your family."

Luon filled my *krama* with food and placed the palm leaf hat she'd made me on my head. I left her stirring the embers. If I stayed any longer, I wouldn't be able to leave. I headed out into the still, dark morning.

Chapter Forty-Five
The Bad Times Come Again

"Stop!" A soldier I'd never seen before blocked the path into Po Kapber Camp. "Show your pass!"

"I live here," I said, shuffling my feet in the dirt.

"Let me see your pass!" he demanded, never taking his eyes off my palm leaf hat.

If he didn't believe me, he would kill me. He could kill me anyway. Slowly, I removed my hat and held it out. He snatched it so fast that his jagged nails scraped my hand. He motioned for me to pass.

I walked through camp, straining to hear familiar sounds. Everything seemed empty. The voices of children playing were gone. The cackling of women doing laundry was gone. There was a line of trucks parked beside the warehouse. I wanted to see if the boys were inside, but I was afraid of the trucks. I went to Mir Tuck's house. A strange woman came to the door.

"Mir Tuck is gone," she said.

Nodding my thanks, I backed away. As soon as I was out of sight, I ran to the kitchen. I was looking for Chinaman. "You're still here," I panted.

Chinaman looked up from the rice he was stirring. Mir Tuck's monkey was perched on his shoulder. "I wonder for how long," he said. And then, as if I'd never been gone, he kept right on talking and stirring. "Did you see the trucks?" he asked. "They're taking the food from the warehouse. They said Mir Tuck and his soldiers were stealing from *Angka*, that others all over Kampuchea are starving while we eat cans of lychee nuts. Are you hungry, *boun*?" Without waiting for an answer, he handed me a bowl.

Mir Tuck's monkey scampered across the table onto my shoulder and began digging in my pockets for a treat. "He remembers me," I said.

Chinaman chortled. "The new leader, Mir Chuk, tried to make friends with the monkey by giving him a piece of mango."

"Did he spit it out?" I gasped.

"Right in his face!" said Chinaman. "I started to choke I was trying so hard not to laugh." Chinaman tugged the monkey's tail. "Good monkey." The monkey climbed onto my head and scolded Chinaman.

A soldier stormed into the kitchen. His uniform was mud-streaked, and his sandals were tied onto his feet with strips of tire tube. "Where's our food!" he demanded.

Chinaman shrugged. "It will be ready when it's cooked." No sooner had the words left Chinaman's mouth than the gun was out of the soldier's holster. Chinaman was thrown against the wall by the blast. I steeled myself to ignore the gaping hole that had been Chinaman's stomach. I felt his hot blood seep between my toes.

"The rice is ready now," said the soldier. "Bring it to us."

Frantically I scooped the rice into bowls.

Mir Chuk made me take Chinaman's place. Several times a day he came by the kitchen to check on me. If he didn't think I was working hard enough, he threatened me with his gold-topped stick. I'd seen the results of Mir Chuk's threats: swollen welts on the backs, arms, and legs of the orphan boys.

After Chinaman was killed, Mir Tuck's monkey wandered around the camp like he was looking for someone. Sometimes when I was cooking, he'd climb into the kitchen and swing down onto my shoulder, picking at my head like he used to and chattering away. I'd scratch him and chatter back.

One day when the monkey was perched on my shoulder, I heard the brakes screech on Mir Chuk's bicycle. I stopped chattering and started chopping furiously.

"Get this ready to cook!" Mir Chuk said as he threw a scaly, reddish brown ball onto the table. "I want to eat it tonight."

I pulled the long rat-tail away from the armor-plated shell and tried to stretch out the pangolin's body.

Mir Chuk rubbed the fur on the monkey's back. "You're the little guy who doesn't like mangoes," he said. "You were Mir Tuck's pet. Maybe you'd like to be my pet now." He reached for the monkey. It clamped its teeth into his hand. "Aiyiiii!" Mir Chuk jerked back his arm and flung the monkey to the ground. Picking up a knife from the table, he sliced open the monkey's chest, carved out the heart, and ate it.

.   .   .

Every night there was a meeting. They were like all the meetings I'd ever been to. Mir Chuk or another leader preached at us. "You have been lazy and idle. *Angka* needs more rice." They told us that Mir Tuck was a traitor to the people. "You have to work harder now so *Angka* won't think you are greedy and corrupt like Mir Tuck." We struggled to stay awake while soldiers marched between the rows, monitoring us.

"Here comes Comrade Ngim," whispered Tek. "Should we wake up Khour?"

"No, let him sleep," said Sok. "We worked hard all day. We should all be asleep instead of having to come to these meetings."

Sok had not had to go to meetings before, so he didn't know how serious they were, but I did. I poked Khour in the ribs. Comrade Ngim started down our aisle. Concentrating on the saliva spraying out of Mir Chuk's mouth, I willed Comrade Ngim to pass us by.

Finally, the meeting was over. Stumbling after the others, I heard Tek whisper, "Stay close together, or the ghosts will get you."

"I bet Chinaman's ghost entered the monkey after they killed him," said Sok. "Let's go see."

"If you poop on a Chinaman's grave, he'll turn into a cat," Mouk whispered through the darkness.

Mouk had taken over as leader of the group because his father was one of the new soldiers. He pushed us around to prove how tough he was. I didn't want to go with him to the graveyard, but I knew if I didn't he'd pick on me.

Every shadow tried to grab us on the way to Chinaman's grave. When we found it, Mouk hissed a string of jumbled words that he said was a charm to call the spirits, pulled his pants down, and pooped on the mound.

For the next several days, whenever any of us had to defecate, we went there. We watched and waited, but we never saw a cat.

About a week later, we were lying on our mats when Sok rushed in shouting, "He's coming! The cat-ghost is coming!" The warehouse began to shake. We cowered in the corners, trembling, until we heard laughter through the floorboards. Mouk was the ghost!

Chapter Forty-Six
House Boy

"Mok!" Wern charged across the road. He hugged my legs, knocking the firewood out of my arms. I let him lead me to his hut. "Ma! Ma! Mok's back!"

Mien Chorb looked up from the mosquito net she was mending. "We thought you were dead," she said. "Mir Chuk's people took Chorb away. They came when we were sleeping and forced him into a truck with other soldiers. They said he needed to be re-educated. They took my wedding dress and my jewelry and all of our food. What will happen to us?" She wept.

I moved back in with Mien Chorb, Khour, and Wern.

Our food allotment was a half can of rice for each person who worked. After a day in the field, I dug roots and set traps to supplement our meager rations. Mien Chorb did her best to make the strange foods appealing, but Wern wouldn't eat.

"Not good," he said when she mixed bits of snake with the rice. He spit out the rubbery, gray grubs and refused to open his mouth to anything except watery rice soup.

When her coaxing and cajoling failed, Mien Chorb cradled Wern in her lap and, using the same method my mother had used to feed me when I was a baby, chewed the food for him and pushed it between his lips.

Wern whimpered constantly, rubbing his distended belly. In order to take his mind off the hunger pains, I brought him a centipede. I pulled off the poisonous part and set the insect beside him. He was so fascinated by the centipede's many legs that he forgot his hunger. For hours he sat quietly while the centipede crawled over his body. Then, one by one, he plucked off its legs. When the centipede lay still and legless, we ate it.

Khour wasn't glad that I had returned. He followed me around just to taunt me. "That's not the way it's done," he shouted when I patched a hole in the roof. "If you want to act like a dog, maybe you should sleep outside," he sneered when I crawled on the ground with Wern on my back. When I carried water from the river, he said, "Next time, clean your ears. I'm tired of having to tell you everything over and over again." Even in the fields, he scolded me. No matter how cruel he was, I smiled and nodded.

One day Khour was being particularly mean. I hid in a bale of hay to escape his jibes and fell asleep. Grunts and groans woke me. The bale rocked. Someone was trying to move it.

"What's the matter, Khour?" teased Tek. Khour moaned. The bale rocked again.

"Can't you move a little pile of hay?" asked Sok.

"This bale's heavier than the others," said Khour.

I saw him peek inside. "Yaaagh!" I screamed, jumping out of the bale. Khour fell backwards. Everyone laughed.

Khour's face burned red. He charged, grabbed me around the waist, and pulled me to the ground. For a moment I let my anger loose and fought back, blocking Khour's hands as he clawed at my face and ripped at my shoulders with his teeth.

Then Khoy flashed before my eyes. *If you win, you lose,* I thought. I made my body go limp and endured Khour's brutal attack.

Chapter Forty-Seven
Caught!

While Mir Tuck had been leader, our belies were kept full by regular hunting trips, a flourishing vegetable garden, and a warehouse full of rice and canned food. After the trucks emptied the warehouse and Mir Chuk cut our rations, the good life at Po Kapber Camp came to an end. We fought like buzzards for every tiny morsel.

Scavenging took me back to the rice paddy in the valley. The rice shafts were tall and green, but the heads had not yet developed. I found a fish trap floating in the paddy. I knew it belonged to someone, but I was so desperate that I didn't care. It had been days since we'd eaten anything except watery rice soup. I picked up the trap. It was empty.

"Hey! What are you doing?" A soldier was running toward me with a bayonet. "That's my trap!"

I dropped the fish trap and ran. The rice plants engulfed me. The soldier followed my muddy trail through the paddy. When I reached dry ground, I stopped. I could hear him splashing after me. I knew I couldn't outrun him. I was too weak. *If he catches me, he'll kill me,* I thought.

I took a few steps out of the paddy, then backed up into my footprints. Turning quickly, I ducked into the water, squatting down so only my head poked out. I prayed that the rice shafts would hide me.

The soldier ran past. He spotted my footprints on the dry ground and followed them. After a minute, he came back. He searched the paddy, passing right next to me. I held my breath. The soldier looked all around but couldn't find me.

Returning with a bounty of paddy crabs, I was stopped by Mien Pha, one of the soldier's wives. "Where have you been?" she demanded.

"I had to pee," I stammered.

"I know all about you," she said. "You sneak off to find food. Then you keep it for yourself. The rest of us are eating watery gruel while you eat meat. I can smell the cooking in Chorb's wife's hut." She squeezed my arms and chest, searching for hidden goodies. With a triumphant yelp, she found the hidden crabs. "You are stealing from *Angka*! I'm going to tell the leaders, and you will be punished."

"Please, please," I begged. "Don't tell. I'll find food for you."

So she took the crabs and let me go.

I told Mien Chorb what had happened.

"Pha is a big-mouth," she mumbled. "We will all be killed."

At the next meeting, when Mir Chuk asked for confessions, Mien Chorb came forward. "I want to be better for *Angka*," she said. "While others go hungry, my children are full. Mok brings us grubs, roots, crabs, and berries to add to our rations."

I was shaking so badly that I wasn't sure my legs could support me. I cleared my throat. "I'm sorry I haven't shared the food I found." My voice wavered. "I want to be a good Khmer. I will show everyone how to find food."

That night and the nights that followed, I showed Mien Pha and the others how to make traps and hunt. One of Mir Chuk's soldiers was always with us. If we caught something good, like a rabbit, the soldier claimed it for *Angka*.

I taught them all of my secrets, afraid that if I kept anything back, I'd be punished. I showed them the best places to forage, taught them about poisonous mushrooms, and showed them how even termites could be a meal. I filled a pot with water and explained how the termites thought the water was a place to build a new colony. Even mean-mouthed Mien Pha smiled as the termites swarmed over the pot and lost their wings diving into it.

Chapter Forty-Eight
Dey Gra Hom

Along with the other boys, I was sent to clear new fields in Dey Gra Hom. The name, meaning "Red Dirt," came from its orangey-red soil. A patch of land had been cleared of trees; only stumps were left. We were ordered to remove the stumps from the dry, crusty ground. Our tools were an ax, a pick, and a *parang*. Mouk claimed the ax. The rest of us took turns hacking at the stumps and pulling the dirt away with our hands.

The dank jungle air pressed in on us. Raising an arm sent rivers of sweat coursing down our bodies. Our thirst was unquenchable. We poked a hole in the trunk of a banana tree and drank the clear, bitter juice. While we worked, we chewed pieces of the tree, rolling the sour, green inner flesh in our mouths, grateful for the little bit of liquid.

When the pile of stumps was as high as our heads, Comrade Ngim ordered me to burn them.

"May I wait till tonight when it's cooler?" I asked.

"No," said Comrade Ngim. "Burn them now."

The flames scorched my face. The sun beat down on my neck and back. I burned, then shivered, burned, shivered. My vision blurred. I leaned against a tree to steady myself.

"Lazy boy!" Comrade Ngim shouted. "If you have time on your hands, I have work for you."

She ordered me to hold a branch over her head while she ate pumpkin soup and roasted bananas. Then she sent me back to the fire.

Stirring the ashes, I turned up a turtle that had been caught in the blaze. I dug the shell from the coals and cracked it open. The turtle meat had been burned to a crisp. There would be no food until evening, when we returned to Po Kapber. Even then, eating came after Mir Chuk's meeting.

Mir Chuk demanded confessions, so we made them. "You must all watch each other and help each other," he said. "If a comrade does something wrong, you must remind him what is right."

Sok jumped up. "Mok has not been helping *Angka*," he said.

A hard ball grew inside my chest.

"When we were planting beans," he continued, "Mok didn't push hard enough on the stick, and his rows were crooked."

They were waiting for me to answer. I stood and faced Sok. "Thank you for showing me how I can do better for *Angka*," I said. "I'm sorry I didn't make straight rows. I was dizzy and couldn't see. I will try harder to make straight rows. I want to plant lots of beans for *Angka*."

Comrade Ngim slammed her fist on the table. "You always say you can't see well or you're sick! Doesn't *Angka* give you enough rice to eat so you can work hard?"

No, I never have enough to eat, I thought, keeping my eyes down. "Yes," I said humbly. *"Angka* gives me more than enough to eat."

"Remember that, and don't be a lazy Lon Nol," she said, writing down my name. "If I see your name on the list again, you will be punished."

I was lucky. The next time someone reported me, Comrade Oan was the leader. He couldn't read, so he didn't know that my name was on the list.

After the beans were in, we planted pumpkins, cucumbers, corn, and watermelon for *Angka*'s garden. Birds flocked to the fields to snatch the seeds. Pelting them with rocks, we killed as many as we could.

Mouk followed one of the birds to its nest and stole the babies. He brought them back to the warehouse and fed them grasshoppers. The baby birds followed Mouk around, cheeping. They thought he was their mother.

"Are you big enough to eat yet?" he asked, squeezing them.

When they were big enough, Mouk ate them!

Chapter Forty-Nine
Wern's Discovery

When the crops were in, we went back to Po Kapber Camp. There, I was drawn to Wern. Being around him made me sad and happy at the same time. I couldn't stop myself from watching as he slept peacefully in bed beside his mother. I knew the love he felt in her arms, pressed protectively against her body, because my mother had been the same with me.

I used any excuse I could find to stay around the hut so I could listen to Mien Chorb croon to Wern and play with him, making up nonsense rhymes and finger games.

As much as I relished the way Mien Chorb cosseted Wern, Khour hated it, jealous of the attention his brother received. At every opportunity he picked on Wern, pulling his hair, tripping him, and tormenting him with stories about ghosts and wild animals that were waiting to steal and eat little boys.

Trying to protect Wern only caused me trouble. I found that out when I made the mistake of defending Wern from Khour's cruelty.

"Get away, idiot boy!" screamed Mien Chorb, hitting me. "You have no business interfering between brothers."

Still, I couldn't stand watching Khour abuse Wern, so under the pretext of helping Mien Chorb, I did my best to keep Wern out of Khour's way. Lonely for his father, Wern happily accepted me as a substitute for Comrade Chorb.

Wern was sitting in the doorway one day when Khour and Im returned from the fields.

"Give me my bath!" Wern demanded. He held his arms out to me.

"He'll just pour water over you like Ma does," said Khour.

"I don't care," said Wern. "I want Mok to do it."

"Sure, let idiot boy give you a bath," said Khour. He picked up a handful of dirt and threw it at me. "And you can wash yourself while you're at it."

Wern chattered all the time I was bathing him. I left him on the riverbank and waded in to fill the pot with cooking water. "Look what I have!" Wern squealed. He was jiggling his penis.

Trying to divert him, I told him about the green mamba snake I'd found coiled in the branches of a mangrove. I thought I'd succeeded when he asked "Did you catch it?" but I was wrong.

"Vathana doesn't have one," he said, marching over to his mother.

"One what?" Mien Chorb looked up from the root she was peeling.

"This!" Wern proudly clutched his penis. "Do you have one, Mok?"

My face red, I dumped the pot of water over him. The next day, Wern was wearing pants.

Chapter Fifty
The Marriage Ceremony

Two or three months later, we were sent back to Dey Gra Hom. Tangled vines heavy with plump pockets of beans covered the field.

"See how well *Angka*'s beans grow," said Comrade Ngim. While she droned on about the glories of *Angka*, I dreamed of running through the field, popping open the pods, and stuffing myself.

"Get to work!" she commanded. "The beans must be harvested before they rot on the vines."

We lined up at one end of the field. Like paddy crabs, we picked our way through the bean plants. The crisp, green smell rushed into my nostrils each time I snapped a pod from the vine. I could hear Mouk next to me, chewing. I was scared. Comrade Ngim was always watching me because I wasn't Khmer Rouge. I wished I could kill her the way Mir Chuk had killed the monkey; then all the beans would be mine. When she turned her head, I shoved a pod into my mouth.

At that moment, Comrade Oan ran into the field, shouting and waving his hands. "Stop what you're doing! Return to Po Kapber!"

The camp was overrun with new people. They slumped against the sides of huts and squatted in the road. About twenty young girls had spread blue tarps on the ground beneath the warehouse. Without speaking, they set about the business of making camp, rolling out sleeping mats and building fires.

Comrade Oan ushered us into the meeting place. Mien Chorb and the other women were already there, seated in rows, glassy-eyed, rocking their swollen-bellied children, suckling babes at their empty breasts.

I heard shouting. The soldiers dragged the girls from under the warehouse and rounded up the rest of the newcomers, arranging them in two rows, boys facing girls. Their arms, stick thin, dangled from the sleeves of their ragged shirts. Backs bowed, their knife-sharp shoulders jutted forward, framing their ravaged faces. Eyes sunken deep in their heads stared out from black-rimmed sockets. *Do I look like that?* I wondered, knowing that I did. We all did.

Hours later, a procession of officers marched in after Mir Chuk and seated themselves behind the table. Mir Chuk rose from his seat. He walked between the boys and girls, waving his walking stick around each pair. When he got to the end, he turned around and faced the couples. "*Angka* decrees that you are married," he announced. "You will have babies so that there will be more people to work for *Angka*."

A terrified girl no older than Saveun dared to meet the eyes of the boy across from her. His lips parted, revealing cankerous gums. A tear slid down the girl's cheek.

I was thankful that I was too young to be married.

Chapter Fifty-One
There Are Traitors among Us

The couples had been brought to Po Kapber to help with the harvest. Like machines, they attacked the field, picking everything—ripe, green, or bug-infested. The officers that had accompanied them were different. They never talked among themselves or lazed around. They stood on the edge of the field, watching, waiting for someone to fall behind so they could use their clubs.

Frightened of the new soldiers, I didn't dare sneak even one bean. But that didn't stop me from thinking about the beans that would be in my bowl at mealtime. After the first few days, however, with only the same watery rice soup to eat, I realized that the vegetables were not for us.

"Food has been stolen from the kitchen," announced Mir Chuk. I'd been concentrating on staying awake, not listening to his propaganda, until I heard the word *food*.

"We've been breaking our backs harvesting crops for *Angka*," continued Mir Chuk. "Now, traitors are stealing food. While we go hungry, their bellies are full. They must be stopped."

My group was assigned to guard the kitchen. Night after night, after working all day in the fields, we watched for the traitors to come, but we saw no one.

At every meeting, Mir Chuk screamed at us to find out who was stealing the food. I saw the way his jowls jiggled when he raved, the way his pudgy arms stretched the sleeves of his shirt. It was clear that he and his soldiers were the thieves.

Curled up in the kitchen between baskets of vegetables, I stopped watching for traitors and let myself fall asleep.

Chapter Fifty-Two
The Vietnamese Are Coming!

"Our crops weren't enough to feed even a handful of *Angka*'s soldiers," announced Mir Chuk. "You must build a dam to catch the water. Then we'll be able to grow two or three crops a year instead of only a measly one."

Rice bowls on our heads, the soldiers marched us over Po Kapber. The married ones, who were sicker and weaker, slowed us down. Some fell along the way. Not wanting to leave them for wolves and buzzards, we half-carried, half-dragged them along.

As we walked south, the trees and bushes disappeared until only the flat, barren plain stretched before us. The red, chapped earth burned through my sandals. I stopped looking where I was going and followed Sok's feet as he plodded ahead of me.

We made camp in the shade of a giant boulder jutting up from the plain. Since there was no wood to make a shelter, we crawled into the boulder's crevices and collapsed.

The next morning we started building the dam. The boulder we were camped under was part of a big, round mountain. Sok said it looked like a chicken egg. Beside it was an even larger mountain that we called Duck Egg. The mountains were covered with rocks. While the soldiers sat and watched, we loaded rocks from these mountains into baskets and lugged them down to where the plain narrowed into a gorge. A basketful at a time, we built a wall across the gorge.

One day, after dumping my load of rocks, I stretched my arms and neck, trying to alleviate the throbbing pain in my back. I looked up at the cliffs rising on either side of the gorge. I looked down at the paltry pile it had taken us a week to gather. *It'll take all the rocks from Chicken and Duck Mountains to build this dam,* I thought.

"Get back to work!" shouted a soldier from his perch in a shallow cave above my head. "If you don't work, you don't eat!"

Our rice had run out, and our water was almost gone. Hard work and burning sun had quickly sapped any strength the married ones had left. Many of them were only able to carry one rock at a time, stopping every few steps to catch their breath.

Because we were the strongest of the weak, my group was sent back to Po Kapber for supplies. I smelled the cooking fires long before we crested the mountain. Driven by hunger, we crawled like spiders down the ridges.

As soon as we entered camp, we knew that something was wrong. Mien Chorb ran out to meet me.

"The Vietnamese are coming!" she cried. "Mir Chuk and his soldiers have left. They took most of the rice and all of the guns. They're going to fight the Viet Cong. You can hear the guns at night. We will all be killed. The Viet Cong hate us. They will cut off our heads!"

My heart leapt. *They won't kill me,* I thought. *I'll tell them I'm half-Vietnamese, and they'll take me back to my mother.* I tried to remember the Vietnamese words, but after four years of making myself forget my Vietnamese half in the camps, the words had disappeared.

Chapter Fifty-Three
Leaving Po Kapber Camp

The only soldiers in Po Kapber were the three who had come back with us from the dam. They took the boys into the rice paddy. Because I was not Khmer Rouge, I was left behind. I followed them and watched from a distance. Using sticks as guns, the soldiers taught the boys how to fight the Vietnamese. Secretly, I practiced their defensive techniques.

We heard shooting all the time. Fires from falling mortar turned the sky orange and sent clouds of smoke billowing up through the valley. Ashes filtered into our food and settled on our hair and eyelashes. A mortar fell onto a haystack and set the warehouse on fire. In the midst of the chaos, the soldiers took everything they could carry and ran away, leaving the rest of us to fend for ourselves.

"The Vietnamese won't kill me!" announced Sok, leading the boy-soldiers out of Po Kapber Camp to confront the enemy. Each of them carried a killing stick.

Mien Chorb pushed me into the hut with Khour and Wern. "Stay here and wait for me," she ordered.

I hadn't known it before, but Mien Chorb had been planning to leave all along. When she came back, she had two chickens stuffed under her shirt. She dug up a hoard of rice, vegetables, and dried fish that she had stashed in a shallow pit under her mat.

We ran as fast as we could away from Po Kapber Camp. I didn't know where we were going. I don't think any of us did. Our only thought was to get as far as possible from the fighting.

It wasn't long before we found the boy-soldiers. They had been bound, blindfolded, and shot. An old man was untying them so they wouldn't go into another world with their hands bound. I wanted to help bury them, but Mien Chorb wouldn't let me.

We ran, and when we became too tired, we walked. The settlements we passed were being deserted; everyone was fleeing from the dreaded Vietnamese. Unlike the evacuation from Small Bor, no one had televisions, refrigerators, or crates full of livestock. No one pushed cars or was dressed in silk sarongs and Western suits. We were all the same: tattered, black-clad skeletons with empty bowls on our heads and a few possessions tied in our *kramas*.

We didn't stop until the mortar fire had faded to a faint rumble. We wandered into a village that was seemingly untouched by the threat of a Vietnamese invasion. The farmers said we could stay if we helped with the sugar cane harvest.

Mien Chorb told the villagers that I was a dumb boy she had saved from the Vietnamese. She bossed me around like I was her slave. She ordered me to build a bomb shelter. I dug the hole chest-deep. While I was cutting banana leaves to cover it, I discovered a deserted pagoda. I went inside, hoping to find something useful. In a corner, under a pile of rubble, I found a sack. It was stuffed with thousands of *riel*. Crumpling the money in my hand, I remembered begging

Luon for just one *riel* to buy ice cream. I remembered selling fruit to pay for the shadow play. I hugged the bag. Someone had hoarded all these *riel*, and it was of no use now because the people were dead, and the money was no good anyway. My tears dripped into the sack.

"What kind of place is Kampuchea?" I cried. "Why am I here?"

I took the *riel* to the river, where I threw them into the air and watched them float away.

Chapter Fifty-Four
1979: Soldiers in Green

About a month later, they came—soldiers in green, marching across the fields in twos and threes, raising dust clouds with their combat boots. Sunlight bounced off their helmets and machine guns.

Mien Chorb cowered in a corner of the bomb shelter. "My head won't be on my body anymore!" she shrieked.

Khour and Wern buried their heads in her lap. I was too terrified to move.

When the Vietnamese soldiers found us, they smiled and said, "*Die yeh.*"

"Go home," I translated. "They want us to go home." But we had no home. We had no food. We headed for Battambang, begging along the way.

"Hey, old woman!" Mien Chorb called to a gnarled figure sitting under a bridge. "Do you have food to trade?"

When the old woman didn't answer, Mien Chorb sent me to wake her. She didn't respond. I nudged her. She was dead.

Mien Chorb rifled through the woman's belongings. She plucked a tiny green stone coated in wax from the old lady's ear. "Take her cooking pot and let's go," she said.

We camped by the railroad tracks about thirty-five kilometers from Battambang. Mien Chorb tried to trade the items she'd taken from the old woman at other camps along the tracks. She returned empty-handed and took her frustration out on me. "Did you find anything to eat while I was gone?"

I pointed to the bamboo shoots, *ptib*, and mushrooms in the cooking pot.

"That's nothing," she said. "The Khmer Rouge have hidden caches of food in the jungle. Instead of sitting here like a lazy Chinese, you should be out looking for them."

"We'll have a better chance of finding the hiding places if we all go," I told her.

"Listen to the dumb boy telling me what we should do!" she spat. "While he eats out of my bowl...," she yelled, punctuating each word with a blow to my back and shoulders, "....who will watch over our valuables? Who will take care of Wern? Get out of my sight!"

●　　●　　●

Each day when I returned without the coveted caches, Mien Chorb screamed and beat me again. She ignored the fact that the roots and berries I found were keeping us alive.

I wasn't alone in my search for hidden food. I roamed in a pack of hungry, homeless souls. We were afraid to go off by ourselves because Khmer Rouge resisters were hiding in the jungle.

Dead bodies were everywhere, foul smelling, putrefying. "These people weren't careful," said one of the men, leading us in a wide circle around some remains. "They stepped on mines. They should have watched where they were going."

A deafening blast cut his words short. The man's legs were torn from his body as the explosion threw him against a tree. We listened to his agonized screams, knowing that there was nothing we could do to stop his pain.

. . .

Soon after that I left the pack, convinced that I would be safer going alone. Besides, our jungle search had been fruitless. I took to combing the riverbanks. I salvaged clothing, rusty cans, and pieces of furniture, most of them too waterlogged to be of use. I was tempted to eat the dead animals and fish that floated by, but I remembered the people at the *wat* vomiting after eating the sick chickens, and I left the carcasses alone. But I couldn't pass up a piece of cowskin. I was so hungry that I assured myself it was safe to eat. I boiled it for a long time. Every so often I chewed on a corner to see if it was soft enough. Two days later, when I returned to camp early, looking forward to eating the cowskin, Mien Chorb, Khour, and Wern were finishing the last of it.

Once a whole crate of batteries washed ashore. The ink on the wrappers was smeared, but the batteries were still good. Mien Chorb traded them for rice.

Sometimes I didn't find anything.

"You're keeping the best for yourself," Mien Chorb accused me. "From now on, Khour will go with you to make sure you bring back everything you find."

Khour relished our forays to the river, away from Mien Chorb's watchful eye. He used the time to pick on me and make mischief.

"Look, a fishing line!" he said, catching sight of a length of twine tangled under a bridge. "Let's see if there's a fish on it."

"No," I said, holding him back. "It might be a bomb."

"It's not a bomb," Khour insisted. "Even if there's not a fish on it, we can use it to fish with."

"I'm scared," I said. "Let's leave it alone. We'll find something better."

Khour glared at me. "If you don't pull it in, I'll tell my mother on you!"

Cautiously, I tugged on the string. It came loose with a click.

"Run!" I yelled. Khour and I dove from the bridge, landing in the swamp grass. Seconds later, the grenade exploded, blowing up a fountain of water, mud, and wood splinters.

"Mok pulled the string!" Khour told the people who rushed over. "He almost blew me up!"

"I didn't want to do it," I protested. "Khour made me."

The crowd pinned me against the riverbank. "Stupid boy! Are you crazy? You could've killed us all!" they screamed, pummeling me.

Chapter Fifty-Five
The Market Is Back

"The market is back," said Mien Chorb. "Those Rot Pun—those smugglers—are bringing food from Thailand. Our neighbor traded her gold tooth to one of them. The Rot Pun gave her rice and sugar for it. Tomorrow morning we are going to Battambang!"

Since I was the only one who'd been to Battambang, I guided Mien Chorb and the boys into the city. The streets, empty when I had left the hospital, now teemed with people. Hollow-eyed children and women cried out to us as we passed by.

We didn't have to ask where the market was; we could smell it. Grilled beef strips and pork, peppers, squash and noodles, and bean cakes and other sweets lured us to the vendors.

Distracted by the colorful packages of Chinese food and spices, we forgot to keep an eye on Wern. For a few nerve-wracking moments, we screamed his name. Finding a small boy in black among a sea of black-clad bodies seemed an impossible task.

Suddenly, Mien Chorb snatched a handful of shirt and jerked back on a dark streak chasing a chicken. "Stay close!" she snapped at the startled Wern. "If you get lost, who knows what will happen to you?" With Wern in tow, she pushed through the crowd of desperate shoppers.

Jittery, decrepit men surreptitiously sneaked trinkets and pieces of gold from their clothing to barter. Bent and scarred women, offering jewels or scraps of silk, fought for an extra condensed milk can of rice.

"Everyone has jewels to trade," the vendors said, scoffing at the green stone Mien Chorb offered them.

"Thieves and liars!" Mien Chorb ranted. "Only five cans of rice they gave me! They steal the food out of my children's mouths!"

Following Mien Chorb out of the city, I remembered when Khoy and I had left Battambang. We had leapt, clothes and all, into a bomb crater—an American swimming pool, Khoy had called it. I wondered if Khoy was still alive.

"Cow!" said Wern. He poked me. "Cow!"

Dung-colored hide hanging in folds across its bony back, a rheumy-eyed cow lolled in the field next to a dilapidated barn.

Mien Chorb scrutinized the cow. Then, purposefully, she walked toward the barn. "This is my cow," she said when an old man emerged. "I owned it before Pol Pot. Give it back to me."

I was sure that the old man wouldn't believe her, but he did. He gave the cow to Mien Chorb!

"What are we going to do with this miserable cow?" complained Khour, tugging on the rope around its neck. "It's so scrawny and sick it can hardly move."

"We'll feed it grass and hay," explained Mien Chorb. "When it's fat, we'll kill it. We'll eat what we can and take the rest to market. A cow is better than jewels."

Mien Chorb was sure that someone would try to steal the cow. She gave me the job of guarding it. Several times a day she ran her hands over the cow's ribs and flanks, but to her, the cow wasn't getting fat fast enough.

"Lazy boy!" she scolded me. "You sleep all day and don't give the cow anything to eat."

"I took the cow to graze by the river. The grass is thick and green there," I explained, hoping to ward off her fury.

"The cow needs hay," she said. "I saw some on my way to Battambang. Go and get it."

I waited until I was sure that the people who owned the hay were asleep. Creeping over to one of the bales, I reached under it to tie a vine around it. My fingers touched something cold and hard. *It's just a rock,* I thought, and hurried on with my task. When I pulled the bale away, however, I discovered that the "rock" was a green metal box. I dragged it into a thicket and pried open the lid. Rows of shiny brand new bullets gleamed in the moonlight.

"Look what I found!" I said as I proudly set the box before Mien Chorb.

"Where's the hay?" she demanded.

"It's full of bullets," I explained. "The soldiers must have left them."

"The cow can't eat bullets!" She hit me and shoved me down.

Early the next morning she carried the box of ammunition to market. That night and for several days, we feasted on more food than I had seen since the strangers in black had come.

· · ·

Once people realized that the Vietnamese weren't going to kill them and the Khmer Rouge soldiers were gone, they began returning home. Some moved into abandoned houses and started farming. Some pushed carts north to Thailand. Others headed south, east, or west back to their birthplaces, hopeful of reuniting with loved ones. At least once a day, someone came with a picture or a story, looking for fathers and mothers, husbands, wives, and children. Girls and boys, freed from the work camps, most of them younger than I, many smaller than Wern, wandered the roads, begging for food. *That could be Pheap or Saveun,* I thought each time Mien Chorb turned one away.

Every day Mien Chorb took Wern to Battambang, where they begged for food.

"I want to go to Battambang, too," Khour cried.

"You're too big," she said. "Nobody will give you food. Stay here and make sure Mok doesn't let anything happen to the cow."

The fields were dry and brown, the river sluggish and muddy. The marsh grasses were cropped too close to graze the cow. "Feel how heavy the air is," I said to the cow, leading it farther and farther away in search of new pastures. "The rains will come soon."

"Why do you talk to a cow?" asked Khour, jumping out at me from behind a tree. "No wonder they call you stupid."

I kept walking, pretending not to hear. Khour wrapped his arms around the cow's neck. "Does it answer you?"

I tugged on the cow's lead, urging it forward. "Take me to Battambang!" Khour demanded.

"No," I said. "I can't leave the cow. It might run away, and then your mother will be angry."

Khour grabbed the rope. "If you don't take me, I'll tell her you're hiding food from us," said Khour.

When Khour and I returned from Battambang, Mien Chorb was waiting for us.

"Look what I found," said Khour, emptying rice from his pockets.

Mien Chorb scraped it into a bowl. "We'll have plenty to eat tonight," she said. "Where did you get it?"

"Mok took me to Battambang, and—"

"Where's the cow?" Mien Chorb glared at me.

"I found some green grass in the hills and left it there," I explained.

"You left the cow for this pitiful handful of rice?" She threw the bowl at me. I ducked. Rice flew everywhere. Mien Chorb grabbed a piece of firewood and waved it menacingly. "Find the cow, you cheap slave, and don't come back till you do!"

But I never found the cow.

Chapter Fifty-Six
Alone in Battambang

"Please, *met*, I'm hungry," I said, holding out my cupped hands to each passerby. When my eyes grew too heavy and my legs too tired to support me, I climbed into a crawlspace below what had once been an elegant, Western-style hotel. Shredded strips of faded red canvas clung to the filigree above the doorway. I ripped some down to use as a blanket.

I was too scared to go to sleep. Opportunists preyed on anyone they thought might be hiding a little gold or silver or even a bit of food. I saw old people, children, and mothers with babies fall victim to these vultures. Even when sleep overtook my body, my mind remained alert to the sounds around me.

Day after day, I roamed the market, scouring the ground for lost kernels of rice, searching the faces for anyone familiar. I kept an eye out for Mien Chorb. No matter how hard it was surviving alone, I wasn't going to be her slave again.

Sometimes I'd spot a girl who looked like Pheap or hear a voice I thought was Luon's. Exhilarated, I'd race over, only to be disappointed.

One day I saw a man balancing a broken chair on his head. He sang as he made his way through the market. His voice reminded me of Veun. I followed him. A few times

I thought I'd lost him. Then I'd catch sight of his green *krama* and push my way through the crowd to get a closer look. The man disappeared into a doorway. I waited for him to come out. *What if it was Veun?* I thought. *Would he recognize me? Would he know where Luon was?*

Sunlight caught the man's face as he emerged from the building. "Veun!" I cried.

Grabbing me by the shoulders, Veun held me at arm's length. He took in every detail, from Gianh's old sandals to the bamboo slashes on my calves to the fishing line I'd tied around my waist to keep my buttonless shirt closed. His examination stopped at my face. "You survived!" he said.

I looked at him, afraid to ask what I most wanted to know.

Veun read the question in my eyes. "Luon has been looking everywhere for you," he said. "I'll take you to her."

Chapter Fifty-Seven
Survivors

Over and over, Luon smoothed my hair, rubbed my face, patted my hands. Pheap and Saveun wrapped their arms around me. Baby Sinoeun, now toddling, squeezed between us. We stood like that for a long time, grateful to be alive and together at last.

An infant's cry interrupted our reunion. "Tha's hungry," said Luon. She crawled into the lean-to and scooped up the screaming child. "Tha was born three months ago. He came too early but is getting stronger."

While Luon fed Tha, Pheap and Saveun asked me about Mir Tuck's monkey and Chinaman. I evaded their questions as best I could, not wanting to spoil the mood. I was relieved when Luon sent them to play.

"After you left, the leaders called a meeting," she said. "They told us that some of us would be leaving Phnom Pong. I was excited to go because they said in the new place we would have more rice and not have to work so hard. When they divided us up, we were not chosen. I begged to go, but Comrade Muy pushed me aside. 'We don't need pregnant women and children,' he said. I watched the lucky ones leave until all I could see was the tops of their heads. Later, I heard they were killed, and we were the lucky ones."

Luon patted Tha absently. "When we first heard the guns," she continued, "our leaders forced us into the jungle. They told us that if the Vietnamese caught us, we'd be tortured and killed. All day we listened to the fighting; at night we lay awake, terrified, while the bombs fell.

"When the fighting was so close we could smell gunpowder, the soldiers rounded us up. 'Run!' my group leader shouted. 'The Vietnamese are coming!' We ran, with the Pol Pots behind us, into the jungle.

"We ran headlong into a Vietnamese patrol. The Pol Pots started shooting. People were screaming, running everywhere. 'Get your pumpkin heads down!' shouted the Vietnamese soldiers, shoving us to the ground. 'Do you want to get shot?'

"We didn't question why the Vietnamese soldiers were helping us. We buried our heads while they chased after the Pol Pots.

"All around me were bodies. My group leader was dead. His wife and child were, too—shot in the back by Pol Pots.

"That night Tha was born."

Luon cooked vegetables and rice she'd been saving, and we celebrated. Memories flooded my mind of feast days in Small Bor when we were all together—Mir Ton, Khoy, friends, and neighbors. Veun played with Sinoeun, and Luon rocked Tha and watched while the girls and I scraped the sides of the pot, licking our fingers. I knew from her melancholy expression that Luon was remembering, too.

Chapter Fifty-Eight
Making Plans

Our lean-to was one of hundreds inhabited by victims of the Khmer Rouge, who, like us, subsisted on handouts. Along with other children, Pheap and Saveun sat by the road so they could wave and cheer when the Vietnamese soldiers passed by. The Vietnamese had saved us from the Khmer Rouge camps and had given us hope for the future.

A jeep, smoke billowing out from under its hood, pulled off the road. Making his way through the clamoring children, the driver stopped at our camp. With gestures and a few Khmer words, he asked for water. When Luon brought it, she surprised him by speaking in Vietnamese. "Is it okay to go back to Vietnam now?" she asked.

He shook his head. "Vietnam's no good," he answered. "There's fighting everywhere. I've had enough fighting. Go to Thailand. In Thailand there's food and medicine. In Thailand there's peace."

Luon started making plans. From the soldiers, she learned that it would take about a month to walk to the Thai border. She figured it would take twice that long with the babies. By begging, we had enough food to keep us alive, but not enough to feed us on the long journey north. We had to think of a way to accumulate food.

"People at the market are trading sugar for rice," said Veun. "If we could find some sugar cane, we could do that, too."

Veun searched until we found a virgin clump of sugar cane deep in the woods. We cut the cane in the morning when it was cool and the ground was still wet so the stalks would be full of juice. We left before dawn, before anyone else was awake, so that no one could follow us and find where the cane was growing.

We mashed the stalks, and Luon boiled the cane juice until all that was left was brownish chunks of crystal. Veun traded the sugar at the market. The stock of provisions, hidden in a pit under Luon's sleeping mat, grew.

Veun also brought back stories of villages ransacked by soldiers, both Khmer Rouge and Vietnamese. Luon was afraid that the soldiers—or the villagers—would find our hidden stores. We took turns guarding the growing pile.

On one of our trips to cut cane, Saveun and I ran into a pack of Khmer Rouge soldiers.

"What are you doing here?" they demanded. "Put the cane down and sit with us."

Saveun and I were shaking with fear. The Pol Pots surrounded us. We knew that if we ran, they'd kill us.

Saveun fell to her knees, put her hands together, and bowed, touching her forehead to the ground. "Please don't hurt us. We're not important."

The Pol Pots forced us to sit down. "Who do you work for?"

"No one," I answered.

"Do you have a gun?"

"No, *met.*"

"Are there Vietnamese soldiers near here?"

"No, *met.*"

The questioning went on for a long time. Finally, after Saveun and I promised not to tell the Vietnamese where they were, the Pol Pots let us go.

When we returned home, Luon made us show the Vietnamese soldiers where we'd seen the Pol Pots. They were gone, but we found a pile of uniforms shoved under some rocks.

"The Khmer Rouge are scared. They take off their uniforms and wear stolen clothes so no one will recognize them," Luon explained, adding the nuts that the Vietnamese had rewarded her with to our hoard.

"Now we can stay here," said Saveun. "We don't have to be afraid of the Pol Pots anymore."

"The Khmer Rouge may go into hiding, but they will never be gone," said Luon. "It will be a long time before the fighting is over. Only in Thailand will we be safe."

Chapter Fifty-Nine

Sinoeun

Sinoeun was an easy baby. She could sit for hours playing with dirt or a rock she found, or a leaf. She had a smile for everyone, but her favorite person was Veun. Whenever Sinoeun saw Veun, she waved her arms and called "Ba, Ba, Ba, Ba, Ba" until he picked her up.

Usually when Veun went to the market, he went alone. But one day, while we were loading the sugar, Sinoeun climbed into the cart. Her face alight with anticipation, she looked up at us. "Noeun go, too," she said, nestling between the bamboo pipes full of sugar.

As always, Sinoeun melted Veun's heart. They set out for the market together.

Born in a Khmer Rouge camp, Sinoeun had never seen such a colorful, busy place as the market. She was so excited that Veun had a hard time keeping her still. While he was trying to trade the sugar, Sinoeun climbed out of the cart and raced into the street. Before Veun could reach her, she grabbed at the wheel of an oncoming bicycle. The driver tried to stop, but he was going too fast. Sinoeun's arm was crushed in the spokes.

By the time Veun got home with Sinoeun, she was unconscious. Luon cut off her bloody sleeve and washed her arm. Veun hovered over Sinoeun while Luon pushed the splintered bones into place and packed moss around the baby's wound. Each time Sinoeun moaned, Veun cringed. I think he felt the pain more than she did.

Veun refused to eat or sleep. He sat at Sinoeun's side, mumbling, "I shouldn't have let her come with me."

After several days, when it was obvious that the wound was not healing, Luon sent me to find the Kru Khmer.

The Kru Khmer spit betel nut on Sinoeun's maimed arm and said magic words over her. Luon paid him with tobacco. When the tobacco was gone, she paid him with our food. To keep us from starving, Pheap, Saveun, and I picked mango flowers and stole sick chickens—the only ones we could catch.

Sinoeun's arm didn't get better. It hung, shriveled and limp, by her side. Listless, she lay on her mat day after day, unable to walk or eat.

"Find some *ptib*!" demanded Veun. "It will help her arm." I knew that the *ptib* wouldn't help Sinoeun's arm, but it made Veun feel better when he succeeded in forcing a bit of it between Sinoeun's blistered lips.

"She needs to go to the hospital," said Luon.

For hours we waited in the crowded clinic. Finally, it was our turn to see the doctor.

"Where's your money?" the doctor asked.

"All we have is a cooking pot, our sleeping mats, and some old clothes," said Luon. "We have no money."

"Medicine is expensive," said the doctor. "No money, no medicine."

Veun pleaded for the doctor's help. "If anything happens to her, I can't go on," he cried.

The doctor turned away.

Out of his mind, Veun raved, saying things he would have been killed for saying if the Khmer Rouge had still been in charge.

That day, Sinoeun died.

Once again we began to stockpile food for the journey north. Veun helped, but his spirit had died with Sinoeun. One day he took a load of sugar to the market and didn't return. Days passed, and there was no sign of him. We went into Battambang to search. We looked everywhere—by the railroad tracks, inside doorways, down alleys. We even searched the riverbanks.

Weeks passed, and the rains started.

"We can't wait for Veun any longer," said Luon. "Soon the roads will be too muddy to travel."

The next morning we loaded our cart and started walking to Thailand.

Chapter Sixty
Checkpoints

We had barely reached the outskirts of Battambang when we saw a crowd of people blocking the road ahead. Luon sent me to see what was happening. The Vietnamese had built a fence across the road. I climbed atop a rusted car and watched. The soldiers were questioning people. Some were allowed to continue; others were turned back. The land on either side of the road was flat and barren. There was no way to avoid passing through the checkpoint.

At the barrier, a soldier stopped us. "Where are you going?" he asked.

Luon pointed north. "To Sisophon," she said.

Saveun and I kept our heads down, afraid the soldier could see in our eyes that we were trying to escape to Thailand. Tha, sitting in the cart with Pheap, chattered away like nothing was wrong. The soldier chucked him under the chin and, with a cursory glance at our belongings, waved us on.

At the next checkpoint, Luon told the soldier that we were going north and started to push the cart past him.

"Stop!" He grabbed the cart. "Are you trying to leave the country?"

"No," Luon said.

"I know you are," he shouted, smacking her.

Repeatedly, he insisted that we were trying to leave Kampuchea. Each time she denied it, he hit her. Finally, he shoved her out of line. "Go back!" he warned. "Don't let me catch you trying to pass through again."

A family took pity on us and carried Luon to their camp. They cleaned her wounds and rinsed the blood out of her clothes. They said we could stay with them. Luon refused. After dark, we sneaked around the checkpoint.

We made it through several more checkpoints. Some were easy, with friendly soldiers who let us pass. When the soldiers denied us passage, we doubled back and waited until the guards changed and tried again.

More than a month had gone by since we'd started walking to Thailand. The farther north we traveled, the more devastating were the ravages of war. Houses lining the highway were riddled with bullets or had been battered and burned in air raids. Rice paddies, thick with thistles, lay fallow, their dikes broken down, victims of shelling and neglect.

The sick and disabled, left behind because their families could no longer carry or feed them, lay among the debris and rotting bodies. At first we shared our food and water because we couldn't bear to hear their cries. Luon soon put a stop to that. "If we feed every grandmother and crying baby, we will soon join them," she said.

Despite her words, Luon couldn't keep herself from picking up abandoned babies, no matter how scab-covered, filthy, and flyspecked. To her, each one was Sinoeun. Even

Tha couldn't help heal the hole that Sinoeun's death had left in Luon's heart. Luon wrapped the babies as best she could with the dirty rags they'd been left in and cuddled them until we pulled her away.

The last checkpoint was a few kilometers outside Sisophon. It was manned by a soldier cleaning his gun.

"Walk straight through," Luon told us. "Pretend you're deaf. Don't stop no matter what he says."

Pheap, Saveun, and I started walking. "Halt!" ordered the soldier.

We ignored him.

"Halt!" He ran up behind us and grabbed my shirt. He started pushing me around and hitting me.

"Leave him alone!" Luon shouted. She was so angry that she screamed in Vietnamese.

I froze when I heard her. What would the soldier do if he thought Luon wasn't Khmer? He didn't seem to notice. He just kept hitting me. Luon grabbed his arm and tried to pull him off. Her yelling attracted the attention of an officer.

"What's going on?" he asked. At the sound of his voice, the soldier released me and jumped back.

"Is this how you treat people?" Luon demanded. "This boy is deaf!"

The officer picked up my *krama* and helped me repack it. "Where are you going?" he asked.

"We're going home," Luon lied, pointing north. "Our farm is over there."

"Okay," he said. "Pass through."

When we were out of sight of the guards, Saveun squeezed Luon's arm. "We're going home!" she cried. "I can't wait to see the farm!"

"We're going to Thailand," I said.

"But Ma said we're going home," Saveun insisted.

"We have no home," said Luon. "The Khmer Rouge forced us to leave the farm, killed your father, and starved our family. This is not our home. Vietnam is a country of war, too. That's why we left. The Viet Cong fight the South Vietnamese, the French, the Americans, and now the Khmer."

"What about our relatives in Vietnam? What about our mother?" I asked.

"We cannot save them if we don't save ourselves," said Luon.

The market in Sisophon was full of merchandise that had been smuggled across the Thai border by Rot Pun. We traded the cart for rice and headed west through the forest.

We passed village after village of death—entire communities slaughtered by soldiers, either Khmer Rouge or Vietnamese. We turned away from the workers who had been murdered, with hoes, cooking pots, and rice huskers still in their hands, stopped seeing mothers rotting with babies in their arms.

At night, packs of wolves preyed on the decomposing corpses. We heard them howling and squabbling over the bones. We walked when it was dark and slept during the day, more willing to take our chances with wild beasts than with soldiers.

The full force of the rainy season was upon us. Even below the canopy of dense leaves, the rain assaulted us. When our rice ran out, we ate trees leaves and gnawed on roots. Tha sucked on a rain-soaked rag because Luon's milk had dried up. We covered our faces with *kramas*; still, gnats, mosquitoes, and biting flies attacked us. Pheap's face and arms were pocked with puss-filled bumps that she couldn't stop scratching, even in her sleep. Drenched and shivering with cold, we struggled onward.

Bands of Khmer Rouge soldiers roamed the forest, along with Vietnamese patrols searching for them and for people like us who were trying to escape. When we heard voices, we hid. We didn't have to worry about Tha revealing our whereabouts; he was too weak to cry anymore.

After long, wet nights of walking, we hunted out a place to rest and hide from the passing patrols. "Up there," Luon whispered, pointing to a hollow in the side of the mountain.

Hand over hand, we climbed the steep hill and crawled into the cave. Pheap screamed and scrambled backwards. The narrow cavity was lined with skeletons; some of the heads still had tufts of hair stuck to them.

"I don't want to stay here," whimpered Saveun. "I'm afraid of ghosts."

"The ghosts of the monks will protect us," Luon said as she gently moved aside a strip of tattered yellowish fabric to make a bed. "This is what remains of them. When the

Khmer Rouge demanded that the monks denounce Buddha, they ran away and hid in caves like this one."

The skeletons, seated with their legs crossed just as I'd seen them sit so often in the *wat*, now seemed to welcome us.

"Rather than deny their faith, they starved themselves," Luon continued. "The monks had more to fear from the living than the dead." She camouflaged the cave's mouth with branches.

Chapter Sixty-One
No-Man's Land

The moon, our guide to Thailand, was hidden in clouds. We wandered for several nights, lost in the no-man's land between Sisophon and the Thai border. Dizzy and weak with malaria, I mindlessly stumbled after Luon, who was carrying Tha and Pheap at the same time.

My legs buckled, and I fell to my knees. "I can't go on," I told her. "Without me, you'll make it to Thailand." I lay with my face in the mud. "Leave me alone. I want to die."

Luon urged me to my feet. "Don't give up!" she commanded. "We're going to make it." With her on one side and Saveun on the other, we struggled on. Helping me over the rugged slopes and lifting me each time I fell quickly used up the little remaining strength they had. Long before daylight, Luon led us to a sheltered spot. As she lay on the damp ground beside me with her hand on Tha's chest to reassure herself that he was still breathing, I believed that even Luon thought we were finished.

Out of nowhere, a young girl of about ten dressed in a flowered sarong appeared carrying a bowl of rice and fish. She set it before us and left without saying a word.

"Who was that?" asked Pheap.

"She must be an angel," said Luon.

The rice and fish gave us the strength to go on.

We stumbled into a Rot Pun camp—one of many hidden in the mountainous jungle. These black marketers—who regularly crossed the Thai border to smuggle rice, salted pork, cigarettes, aspirin, throat lozenges, and brightly colored fabric into Kampuchea—took pity on us. They fed us and let us dry off by their fire. There were other refugees in the camp who had gone there hoping that they had enough money or jewels to pay the Rot Pun to lead them across the border.

Surreptitiously, I examined the smugglers. Armed with AK-47s, they wore a mixture of Vietnamese, Thai, and Khmer uniforms. I was sure that the Rot Pun had taken these uniforms from soldiers they'd killed. Just as I knew that knives were concealed in their trouser legs, I knew that they'd kill us if we tried to follow them without paying.

Every few nights, a group set out for the border. After they left, we listened for gunfire. If we didn't hear any, we knew they'd made it to Thailand. If we did, we waited for any survivors to return. Often, stories came back of one or two casualties or even a whole group caught in crossfire between Khmer Rouge and Vietnamese soldiers.

"We have nothing to pay a Rot Pun," I whispered to Luon while we listened for the guns. "Maybe we should go back to Sisophon, where we can work and beg until we get enough money to try again."

Luon took my hand and pressed a red jewel into my palm. "I saved this for our escape."

Four years of starving, being beaten, and being forced to work like water buffalo in the rice paddies; four years of watching everyone around us suffer and die. For four long years, Luon had kept that tiny stone—one I'd watched her pry from a broach that Mir Ton had given her—for this moment.

"You knew we'd survive," I said, closing my hand around the gem.

"I prayed that we would," she answered.

We went from one Rot Pun to another, trying to find one willing to take us.

"Four of you and a baby for only one tiny ruby?" they scoffed. "Why should we bother, when others pay gold bars and necklaces full of jewels to get to Thailand?"

We'd almost given up hope when one of the Rot Pun agreed to let us join his group. The first thing he did was collect his fee and check everyone's *krama*. "You can't move fast carrying all this stuff," he said, throwing cooking pots, extra clothes, and sleeping mats into a pile.

Without removing the cigarette from the corner of his mouth, he gave us instructions. "The trail we're taking is an overgrown oxcart path," he said. "It's pretty safe. Most of the mines have already exploded. The bodies will tell you where they were." His wicked laugh made me shudder.

He took the gun from his shoulder and checked the chamber. "The jungle is patrolled by soldiers with bullets to waste. The Vietnamese and Khmer Rouge will kill you. If the Thai catch you, they'll send you back. I'll lead. The rest of you follow, one by one. Don't bunch up."

A baby cried. The Rot Pun glared at the infant. "Whatever you do, keep quiet. All a patrol needs to hear is a kid squalling, and they'll start shooting." A woman clamped her hand over the baby's mouth.

The Rot Pun flicked his cigarette stub to the ground. "We'll leave as soon as it's dark."

Not far from camp, we met up with another group. They were obviously upset, all talking at once. Our Rot Pun went over to speak to them while we waited anxiously, wondering what was wrong.

Suddenly, out of the shadows, a patrol swooped down on us. It was too dark to see whether they were Vietnamese or Khmer Rouge. When they started shooting, people scattered, screaming.

Luon turned and ran.

"Ma! Wait!" shouted Pheap and Saveun, racing after her. Luon yelled for them to lie down. I dove under a tree. From where I was, I could see Pheap and Saveun. They lay motionless in the tall grass, their faces pressed against the ground as beams from the soldiers' flashlights scanned the area.

Help us get out of here, I prayed.

Finally, the guns were silent. When we were sure that the soldiers had gone, we got up. All around us, injured people cried out for help, but the Rot Pun had vanished.

"My wife's been shot!" a man shouted. "I'm taking her back to camp."

Some people left with the man, but most stayed, waiting for the Rot Pun to return.

"Lousy Rot Pun has no race!" said Luon. "He has our money. He won't be back. We'll have to find Thailand without him."

Chapter Sixty-Two
Run for Your Life

Somewhere in the tangled jungle, we lost the oxcart path. For hours we wandered in the dark, searching for signs of a trail.

"It's no use," said Luon. "We'll wait for morning to go on."

At first light, we retraced our steps until we found a path. There wasn't a bird calling or an animal rustling, but we weren't alone. Sometimes we'd glimpse a shirt or a trouser leg, hear a noise or a soft cough. After making sure it wasn't a soldier, we continued, walking on as quietly as we could.

As the jungle thinned, the spaces between the trees widened, and the going became even more treacherous. To choose a path from tree to tree, we first examined the ground for traces of mines and booby traps. We looked for decaying carcasses where unlucky souls had made the way safe for us.

I eyed the distance between trees. Squinting to catch the sun's reflection on a rifle barrel, straining to hear the smallest sound, I sucked in my breath, crouched low, and bolted to the next tree. And the next. And the next. Until I ran out of trees.

Vietnamese, Khmer, or Thai soldiers, not wanting anyone to escape from Kampuchea, had burned a strip of land along the border and lined it with barbed wire. A cratered, gray minefield stretched before me, littered with broken, red-splotched bodies that would be our stepping stones to freedom.

Luon slumped against me. We looked beyond the gray to an endless expanse of green. "That's Thailand," she whispered with a tired smile.

We huddled together as daylight faded. Sporadically, daring souls darted into the open, zigzagging through the maze of mines. Scattered gunfire traced their paths. The moans of the wounded cautioned us as we waited in the dusk.

An old woman carrying a child tripped. Reality exploded in our faces, along with bits of bodies and clothing. Though the night was warm, I was cold with fear.

Finally, it was time—the time between dark and when the moon rises.

"Remember, step only where the bodies are," said Luon, gently smoothing the scars on Saveun's neck.

Luon tied Pheap onto my back. I tightened the *krama* that held Tha onto hers. We didn't have to worry about Tha betraying us; he was still too weak to cry.

"Keep your head down," said Luon, squeezing my shoulder. "We'll be right behind you. Don't stop until you're in Thailand."

My heart pounding, I took a deep breath and ran.

Epilogue

The minefield separating Cambodia from Thailand was only about a kilometer across—not even a mile—but for Mok, it was the longest run of his life. Luck was with him that night. After safely leading Saveun across the field, Mok, with Pheap still tied to his back, followed the barbed wire, searching for the gap in the fence. Once through the fence, he and his cousins were in Thailand, but they were not yet safe. They were still too close to the Cambodian border. Vietnamese and Khmer fighters in Cambodia might still shoot them. And Thai soldiers patrolling the borders might mistake them for smugglers or soldiers in the darkness.

Without stopping to be sure that Luon and baby Tha were following, Mok and Saveun hurried on. Moving as quickly and silently as possible, Mok led the way up a narrow track that wound through the jungle. Gradually, the eerie silence of war lifted, replaced by the sounds of birds calling, dogs barking, people talking and laughing. Reassured by the normality of the sounds, Mok doubled his pace. He didn't stop running until they reached a market.

"It was so odd," Mok recalls, "being so frightened one minute and the next to stumble into this noisy place full of well-dressed people buying and selling everything imaginable. One vendor was even selling ice cream."

Along the border between Thailand and Cambodia, relief organizations had set up camps to care for refugees fleeing the war. Mok and his cousins joined a line of refugees and headed for the nearest of these camps.

In the refugee camp they were given food, basic medical attention, and a place to sleep. "Sleeping shelters made of sarongs were all around the camp," Mok remembers. "Some people slept on the bare ground or on blue plastic tarps; some had strung hammocks between trees and slept there. I led my cousins to a slight hill with a tree on the top. While they slept, I sat with my back against the tree, enjoying my full belly."

Unsure who in the camp they could trust, Mok's family kept to themselves. While most of the refugees were survivors of the horrors of the past four years, wanting only food to eat and a place to live in peace, others were Khmer Rouge who had fled from the Vietnamese. The Red Cross workers, being mainly Westerners, were unable to distinguish between the different groups, so they treated everyone the same.

After Mok and his family had been in the camp for about a month, soldiers from the United Nations moved them to Khao-I-Dang, a permanent refugee camp that the United Nations had established. Khao-I-Dang was a city made of blue plastic shelters. Mok's family was given some blue plastic tarps and assigned a place to live. They made a tent from the tarp and slept inside it, just like the other people. It was hot and stuffy inside the tents, so Mok spent as much time as possible outside. A chain-link fence surrounded the camp to keep the refugees inside.

At Khao-I-Dang, each family was given food, vegetables, and rice, and they each had their own cooking pots—a treat after the communal kitchens of the Khmer Rouge. Doctors took care of them, and before long, with food to eat and medical attention, the cuts and scratches on their bodies healed. Schools were set up in the camp, too. Slowly, the children of war whom Pol Pot and his followers had dehumanized came back to life. They learned once again how to run and laugh and play.

For the first time, Saveun and Pheap attended classes. Mok enjoyed school, but he was not a good student, and the teacher was a stern taskmaster. Each time Mok made a mistake, he got his hands smacked. He was so afraid of making mistakes that he was afraid to try. Finally, out of frustration, he decided to teach himself to read. He pulled a notice off a bulletin board and sneaked it home. Night after night he studied the notice until he was finally able to figure out all the words. As Mok learned to read, his confidence returned, and before long he was taking music lessons and art classes in addition to regular school.

Months stretched on, and the family grew used to life in Khao-I-Dang, but they couldn't stop wishing for their own home and a normal life. Luon asked about obtaining Thai citizenship, but that was not allowed. The government of Thailand was worried that if they started letting the refugees move into the country, it would soon be overcrowded and create political problems.

Luon learned all she could about what was going on inside Cambodia and Vietnam. She longed for news of peace, but it was not to be. The Vietnamese maintained control of Cambodia, but they were still fighting with the Khmer Rouge, whom they had driven back into the mountains and forests. Mok's hope of returning to Vietnam and being reunited with his mother vanished.

What the Vietnamese soldiers whom they had met in Cambodia had told them was true: South and North Vietnam were still in conflict. The best hope for Mok and his family was to find someone in the United States who would be willing to sponsor them. In the United States, they would be safe and free.

In order to secure a sponsor, a photograph of the family was taken and sent to America. Every day Mok checked the bulletin boards, hoping to find his family's name on the list of lucky refugees for whom sponsorship had been secured. Finally, after two years in Khao-I-Dang, his prayers were answered. Thanks to the efforts of the United States Catholic Conference, a parish in Oklahoma had agreed to sponsor the family. In 1981, Mok, his sister Luon, and his cousins Saveun, Pheap, and Tha boarded an airplane bound for their new home in America.

Mok's love of art, fostered in the Khao-I-Dang refugee camp, led him to become a professional draftsman. Married and the father of three, Mok, now a U.S. citizen, lives in Oklahoma. In 1993, for the first time since the strangers in black had marched into his life, Mok was reunited with his mother in Vietnam.

From 1975 until 1979, while Pol Pot and his Khmer Rouge fighters ruled Cambodia, almost two million men, women, and children—one in five Cambodians—were executed or died from disease, overwork, or starvation.

In April of 1998, Pol Pot, whose real name was Salothar Sar, died of a heart attack. The Cambodian government set up a tribunal to bring other senior leaders of the Khmer Rouge to justice. But only a few people have ever been convicted for the atrocities of the Khmer Rouge regime.

Glossary

Angka: "organization," the name for the ruling body of the Khmer Rouge

Angkor: refers to Angkor Wat, the divine temple

Ba: Father

Battambang: the capital city of Battambang Province in northwestern Cambodia

Big Bor: a province in northwestern Cambodia, also known as Pailin Province, located on the border of Thailand and surrounded on the north, east, and south by Battambang Province

boun: "balloon"

Caynau Pole: a bamboo pole that is decorated for Tet, the Vietnamese New Year

cyclo-pousse: a three-wheeled bicycle

Dey Gra Hom: meaning "Red Dirt"

die yeh: "go home" in Vietnamese

gor: a tree whose crushed leaves were used as folk medicine

Hmong: a tribe of people who live in the mountains of Cambodia

kai: a plant with leaves that are used as tobacco

Kampuchea: the name of Cambodia in the Khmer language

Khmer: the people and language of Cambodia

Khmer Rouge: the Revolutionary Army of Democratic Kampuchea

kim chee: pickled cabbage

krama: a large multi-purpose square of cloth used as a head covering, a carry-all, and a blanket

Kru Khmer: a medicine man

ktamtat: a tree whose seed pods were used as a worm cure

Lon Nol: President of Cambodia's Khmer Republic, March 14, 1972, to April 1, 1975; staged a coup d'etat on March 18, 1970, that ousted Prince Sihanouk; permitted the United States to operate on Cambodian territory against the Vietnamese and Viet Cong; became President of the Khmer Republic on March 14, 1972; on April 1, 1975, with Khmer Rouge insurgents only a few miles from the capital, he left the country; died in 1985 in Fullerton, California

Ma: Mother

met: friend, comrade

Mien: Mrs. or Mr.

mir: uncle

parang: a long knife used to cut bamboo

phnom: "hill"

Phnom Koy: Knot Mountain

Phnom Penh: the capital of Cambodia; the name means "the hill of the Lady Penh"

Phnom Pong: Little Mountain

Po Kapber: a mountain named for the crocodile

Pol Pot: leader of the Khmer Rouge

Pol Pots: slang name for Khmer Rouge soldiers

Prince Sihanouk: King of Cambodia in 1941; went into exile in Thailand in 1952; re-entered Cambodia when it was independent in 1953; in March, 1955, he abdicated in favor of his father; at the death of his father in 1960, he was elected Head of State but was overthrown in a coup in 1970; when the Khmer Republic fell in 1975, he became Head of State again; was reinstated as King of Cambodia in 1993

ptib: a spinach-like plant

riel: the currency of Cambodia

Rot Pun: smugglers

rouge: red, the international color of communism

sampeih: a deep bow from the waist; a sign of respect; a greeting

sampot: a knee-length wrap-around skirt worn by both men and women

sdow: a tree whose leaves were used as a folk remedy for malaria

sen: one hundredth of a riel (the currency of Cambodia); essentially the equivalent of a penny as compared to a dollar

Siem Reap: the capital city of Siem Reap Province in northwestern Cambodia

Srai Bun Jul: Four Row Rice Paddy, a children's camp

tekah: a type of lizard

Tet: the Vietnamese New Year

travois: a frame slung between trailing poles and pulled as a conveyance for goods and belongings

wat: a temple; a Buddhist place of worship

Bibliography

Becker, Elizabeth. *When the War Was Over.* Simon and Schuster, 1986.

Bunting, Eve. *The Happy Funeral.* Harper and Row, 1982.

Canesso, Claudia. *Cambodia.* Chelsea House, 1989.

Carrison, Muriel. *Cambodian Folk Stories.* Charles E. Tuttle, 1987.

Casey, Robert. *Four Faces of Siva.* Bobbs-Merrill Co., 1929.

Coburn, Jewell Reinhart. *Khmers, Tigers, and Talismans.* Burn, Hart & Company Publishers, 1981.

Constable, George, editor. *China.* Time-Life Books, 1984.

Crawford, Ann Caddell. *Customs and Cultures of Vietnam.* Charles E. Tuttle, 1966.

Crew, Linda. *Children of the River.* Dell Publishing, 1989.

Criddle, Joan D., and Teeda Butt Mam. *To Destroy You Is No Loss.* Doubleday, 1987.

Crossette, Barbara. "After the Killing Fields." *The New York Times Magazine*, 26 June 1988, section 6, p. 17.

Edmonds, I. G. *The Khmers of Cambodia.* Bobbs-Merrill Co., 1970.

Erlanger, Steven. "The Endless War." *The New York Times Magazine*, 5 March 1989, section 6, p. 24.

Fiffer, Sharon Sloan. *Imagining America.* Paragon House, 1991.

Freeman, Michael, and Roger Warner. *Angkor.* Houghton, Mifflin and Company, 1990.

Garrett, Wilber E., editor. "The Temples of Angkor: Will They Survive?" *National Geographic*, May 1982, p. 548.

Hsiao, Ellen. *A Chinese Year.* M. Evans and Co., 1970.

Jackson, Karl D., editor. *Cambodia 1975-1978: Rendezvous with Death.* Princeton UP, 1989.

James, Ian. *Inside China.* Franklin Watts, 1989.

Keeley, Edmund. *A Wilderness Called Peace.* Simon and Schuster, 1985.

Kuckreja, Madhavi. *Prince Norodom Sihanouk.* Chelsea House, 1990.

Levin, Claudia, and Lawrence R. Hott. *Rebuilding the Temple: Cambodians in America.* Oklahoma Educational Television Association, 1991.

Livo, Norma J., and Dia Cha. *Folk Stories of the Hmong.* Libraries Unlimited, 1991.

MacDonald, Margaret Read, editor. *The Folklore of World Holidays.* Gale Research, 1992.

May, Someth. *Cambodian Witness.* Random House, 1986.

Ngor, Haing. *A Cambodian Odyssey.* Macmillan Publishing Company, 1987.

Nguyen, Lucy Hong Nhiem, and Joel Halpern. *The Far East Comes Near.* U of Massachusetts P, 1989.

Nguyen, Tiffany. Personal interviews. 12-14 May 1993.

Picq, Laurence. *Beyond the Horizon.* St. Martin's Press, 1989.

"Pol Pot's Lifeless Zombies." *Time Magazine*, 3 December 1979, p. 55.

Ponchaud, Franois. *Cambodia Year Zero*. Holt, Rinehart and Winston, 1977.

Pran, Dith. "Could the Vietnamese Withdrawal Bring Back Cambodia's Nightmare?" *The New York Times*, 1 January 1989, section 4, p. 1.

Pran, Dith. "Return to the Killing Fields." *The New York Times Magazine*, 24 September 1989, section 6, p. 30.

Ross, Russell R., editor. *Cambodia: A Country Study*. United States Government, 1990.

Schanberg, Sydney H. *The Death and Life of Dith Pran*. Penguin, 1985.

Shawcross, William. *The Quality of Mercy*. Simon and Schuster, 1984.

Sheehy, Gail. *The Spirit of Survival*. Morrow, 1986.

Sihanouk, Norodom. *War and Hope*. Random House, 1980.

So, Mony. "Life in Kampuchea since the Communist Takeover in 1975." Paper presented at Tulsa Junior College, 1986.

So, Mony. Personal interviews. Oct. 1988-Jan. 1994.

Spagnoli, Cathy. *Judge Rabbit and the Tree Spirit*. Children's Book Press, 1991.

Szymusiak, Molyda. *The Stones Cry Out*. Hill and Wang, 1986.

Webber, Elsie. *The Saving Rain*. Branden Publishing Company, 1989.

Yathay, Pin. *Stay Alive, My Son*. Macmillan Publishing Company, 1987.